Tempoı Residents

Tax Traps & Planning Opportunities

Steve Parnham

Steve Parnham © 2016

Published by Steve Parnham at CreateSpace

ISBN-13:978-1539647607

Disclaimer

Please note that this book is intended as general guidance only for individual readers and does not and cannot constitute accountancy, tax, legal, investment or any other professional advice. The author accepts no responsibility or liability for loss which may arise from any person acting or refraining from action as a result of anything contained in this book.

The tax legislation and practice of HM Revenue & Customs is constantly changing and evolving. You are recommended to contact a suitably qualified tax adviser, solicitor, accountant, independent financial adviser or other professional adviser for tax, legal, accountancy, financial or other advice. Such an adviser will issue you with a letter of engagement specifically tailored to your needs and request the necessary information and details of your circumstances from you. You should also be aware that your personal circumstances will invariably vary from the general examples given in this book and that your professional adviser will be able to give specific advice based on your personal circumstances.

This book covers UK taxation and any references to 'tax' or 'taxation' in this book, unless the contrary is expressly stated, are to UK taxation only.

CONTENTS

Preface

It tends to be those arriving in the UK who proactively seek tax advice rather than those who are leaving these shores. In a way that makes perfect sense. After all, if you are leaving the UK surely the point is that you will no longer have to pay UK tax or have obligations to report income and gains in the country you are departing from? That very obvious common sense mindset will firmly push thoughts about residence status and UK tax planning towards the bottom of most people's list of 'things to do' for those preparing to move abroad for whatever reason. It may not even get done. This was not the case for a childhood hero of mine.

Way back in the 1960's my favourite band was the Dave Clark Five. Dave Clark subsequently made a lasting contribution to UK tax law when his non-residence arrangements were tested in the well known case of Reed v Clark. For those who would like to delve further into this have a look at Reed v Clark [1985] STC 323, 58 TC 528 but I would do that some other time should you feel the need ... and keep reading.

By the late 1960s and into the 1970s, high rates of income tax, famously mourned by the Beatles in their 1966 recording of "Taxman" on the "Revolver" album prompted many actors, comedians and performers of the day to leave the UK for relatively short periods of time. These 'national treasures' usually seemed to turn up again after a year or two. You will have heard of most of them unless you are in your teens. They were, and to some extent still are, household names. Although Dave Clark was really prominent in the 1960's his classic hits such as 'Bits and Pieces' & 'Glad All Over' were rediscovered by late 1970's punk rock and a deal was signed with Polydor for $450,000 for his back catalogue. An absolute fortune in those days. This deal gave rise to what amounted to considerable trading profits taxable within the UK and, under the rules then pertaining in the UK, Dave Clark would have been liable to income tax on his profits in the year following that in which the profits were made.

As it transpired Dave Clark left the UK on 3rd April 1978 and returned to the UK on 2nd May 1979 without having sold his London flat which he no doubt regarded as his long term home. Dave Clark therefore spent 13 months outside of the country, 13 months which spanned a complete UK tax year, and he did not visit the UK at all during that period.

The big question was whether he was UK resident in the year of absence, the 1978/1979 tax year covering the year ended 5th April 1979. The Inland Revenue, as HM Revenue & Customs were then known, naturally argued that Dave Clark had remained UK resident in the 1978/1979 tax year and therefore that he was fully taxable on his profits in the UK. On the face if it they had a good case and the considerable tax at stake made it well worth their while pursuing the matter.

However, Dave Clark successfully demonstrated that he had not been UK resident in 1978/79 because he had relocated to Los Angeles for a year of non-residence and for a period covering an entire UK tax year. He could also prove it.   By doing this, he hoped to avoid paying income tax on his previous year's income; importantly Dave Clark established that he had acquired a settled way of life in the United States and therefore must be both resident and ordinarily resident (a term which is today largely of historical interest) there.   If this were correct it would require an astonishingly good argument on the part of the Inland Revenue to suggest that he was nevertheless still resident in the UK under the then legislation.

Ultimately, it was decided that what amounted to Clark's sabbatical in the USA did comply with what was then section 108 of the Income and Corporation Taxes Act 1970 (which has since been repealed, of course), and he won his case. It is a case which is often cited for the principle that complete absence from the UK, if coupled with an appropriate span of time, is a reliable way of not being resident in the country for tax purposes.

I said that on the face of it the Inland Revenue potentially had a good case.   It is often forgotten that the outcome was far from a foregone conclusion.   There were a quite a few tax cases, mainly involving mariners, where the courts concluded that the appellants were UK resident however long they had been away from UK shores.   My favourite is the 19th century case of Rogers v IR.   Mr Rogers was a sea captain who left the UK in 1877 on the St Magnus for the East Indies.   Spookily, he was assessed to income tax in 1878/1879, exactly 100 years before Reed v Clark. He retained a home in Innerleven, Fife.   Mr Rogers had no house elsewhere and so it was found that his absence must be temporary and that, as he must be resident somewhere that somewhere must be in the UK. That may seem very similar to Dave Clarke's position but it can easily be distinguished from that case because Mr Rogers could not argue that he was resident in another identifiable country; Dave Clark could and he was correct to do so.

Much has changed since 1878/1879 and even 1978/1979 so it will be fascinating to see how Dave Clark would have fared under the tax regime which has been in force since 6th April 2013 given similar circumstances. We will return to Dave Clark in some of the following chapters.

Just as Dave Clark assumed as he departed these shores in the spring of 1978, this book assumes that the reader will be, or already is, non-resident. This book explains the concept of temporary non-residence, what it is, why it exists and how it might affect you and, if it does, what you can do about it.

In the process it will set out the bare bones of what non-residence means today through the statutory residence test (commonly known as SRT), but it is not a book on the statutory residence test itself. That would require a much mightier tome and it would be a tome running to several hundred pages but the exercise is nevertheless important.

For those not familiar with Dave Clark or his band, the group sold more than 100 million records and scored 15 consecutive top 20

U.S. hit singles between forming in 1962 before disbanding in 1970.

The Dave Clark Five made a record-breaking 18 appearances on "The Ed Sullivan Show," with its weekly audience of 70 million viewers - more than any other band.

Whether you like their music or not, or are even aware of it, one thing which really distinguished them from almost all of the iconic groups of the time is that the band, and Dave Clark in particular, owned all rights to their music. The masters, the bands intellectual property, were only ever leased for periods of about five years.

Smart!!!

Steve Parnham

June 2016

Introduction

HM Revenue & Customs have always been keen to maintain that people remain UK resident for tax purposes despite going abroad on one of two grounds. The first is that they have never in reality left the UK for tax purposes despite spending most of their time overseas. The second is that their continuing links with and visits to the UK compromise their overseas residence status. HM Revenue & Customs have a reasonably successful track record when it comes to challenging individuals versions of events on these grounds.

Before the introduction of the statutory residence test tax advice to individuals considering moving overseas could often leave them worried that, however much they may have thought that they were now overseas, if they were to ever so briefly return and find themselves using a UK mobile phone to arrange a game of tennis or badminton at their (former, of course) local UK sports club with their UK dentist (former, of course) and a pint in their (former, of course) local pub, they could risk HM Revenue & Customs treating them as though they had never left. These sorts of fears led to considerable uncertainty for individuals and their advisers.

Since 6th April 2013 the statutory residence test, a set of statutory tests, have made it much easier to establish your residence status. Your residence status under these rules must be determined separately for each tax year.

The statutory residence test brings with it greater certainty but that certainty comes at a price. Certainty places a clear premium on your actions and the accuracy of your records. To be certain of your status you really need to adopt a 12 year mindset. Why that mindset is required becomes clear as you read each chapter and I will bring together the crucial components of that mindset in the final chapter.

The legislation dealing with the statutory residence test and the temporary non-residence rules is found in Finance Act 2013, Schedule 45. Although I have not undertaken a word count of that legislation I estimate that the 53 pages of densely packed rules probably contain around 25,000 words ... and that is the dry statement of rules without any elaboration of their consequences or any interpretation. About the same length as this book in fact!

The very useful guidance on their interpretation of the legislation provided by HM Revenue & Customs is found in Guidance Note RDR3 and, although more accessible than the legislation, itself runs to 109 pages. As things stand, the fourth and latest version of HM Revenue & Customs Guidance Note on the statutory residence test was published on 20th December 2013. I will make reference to that Guidance Note throughout the book and you may wish to dip into it from time to time for reference purposes. Why? It is HM Revenue & Customs interpretation of Finance Act 2013 ... and they will be calling the shots.

If you are looking for a definitive guide to the minutiae of rules, regulations and HM Revenue & Customs practice covering every particular point and its innumerable knock on effects then given the size of the legislation you would be looking for a book 10–15 times the length of this one and costing between £100 and £250. They exist. You would also have to be willing and able to devote a considerable amount of time to reading it and to fully understanding its contents. Most people will not do this … and rightly so. They have lives to lead. That is, I would suggest, the sort of book which is written with your professional adviser in mind and even then its usefulness would mainly be one of reference. Few people would read a book of that type from cover to cover even if they are professionally qualified.

We, on the other hand, are looking at how the tax planners mind works. This book therefore provides you with an overview of the position from a practical perspective but it is also one which strives to provide you with an insight into the tax planners mind. In so doing it will provide the insight together with sufficient knowledge to enable you to have an informed and productive dialogue with your professional adviser; one which should lead to the personal and practical guidance you need without getting bogged down or lost in the inevitable minutiae.

When you put down this book the question to ask is, 'Can you see the world of temporary non-residence through a tax planners eyes?' not whether you know everything there is to know about the subject. That level of knowledge is the province of your professional adviser who will have many years of knowledge and experience of dealing with the issues in some depth.

The point I am making is that there is no quick or easy way to understand everything about the legislation and its implications but there is a relatively quick way to enable you to effectively liaise with your professional adviser who will doubtless have at least one of the reference books referred to above on his or her bookshelf as well as the experience to factor in the detail of your particular circumstances. You are not Mad Max or any other example set out in this book; everyone's circumstances are unique.

Despite the change in rules in April 2013, the enthusiasm of HM Revenue & Customs for maintaining that individuals remain UK resident despite spending most of their time overseas has not diminished. To some extent, this is reflected in many aspects of the new rules. What has changed is that, if fully understood, the new rules do allow you to anticipate and predict when you are non-resident and whether you are within or outside of the temporary non-residence rules .... provided there is clarity regarding your past actions and future intended actions. Otherwise, you may just find that UK residence has an 'adhesive' quality. What I mean by this in practice is illustrated by another famous tax case which heads up the next chapter.

But why is residence status important? That is simple. Your residence status will be the main, though not the only, factor in determining your continuing liability to UK tax and your obligations to report income and gains to HM Revenue & Customs.

Here is the thing though!

The tax treatment for all capital gains and certain kinds of income does not change if you are only temporarily non-resident – essentially where you are away for a period of five years or less – whatever your actual residence status under the statutory residence test may be.

The next few chapters will look at the statutory residence test and the temporary non-residence provisions. If you have not come across these ideas before I recommend a brief look at each chapter and then be prepared to give them a more thorough subsequent read. You may even have to give them several reads before they make practical sense. That is ok. While each component part makes sense on its own it is the way in which the various component parts interact with the others which leads to the greater complexity which undoubtedly now exists.

If you are familiar with the statutory residence test and temporary non-residence I still recommend that you read each chapter simply to check that we are using the same rules and assumptions.

As a former senior partner of mine once said many, many years ago, "Assume nothing in tax."

Timeless advice!

SECTION 1 – THE STATUTORY RESIDENCE TEST

Chapter 1 – The Context

Planning well in advance of departure from the UK is strongly recommended and anyone using HM Revenue & Customs guidance should bear in mind that the rules are still relatively new and that the guidance could and probably will be subject to change as the new system settles in.

The consequences of becoming non-UK resident have not changed though.

The general rule if you become non-resident is that while you will pay tax on your UK income you will not normally be liable to UK tax on your overseas income. So if you are employed, you will not pay UK tax in respect of remuneration for duties performed abroad. Earnings for duties performed in the UK will remain taxable unless they are only incidental to the overseas duties.

If, however, you remain UK resident despite going abroad, you will pay income tax on all your income whether it arises in the UK or overseas. If you are employed, you will therefore pay income tax regardless of where your duties are carried out.

It is possible that some of your income could be taxable in the UK and also taxable in the country that you have moved to. However, the worst case scenario is that you will effectively end up paying just the higher of the UK tax or the tax charged abroad. It is important, however, that you take local advice when moving abroad about the tax rules that will apply in the country where you will be living.

If you are UK resident then you will pay UK capital gains tax on gains from disposing of your assets wherever they are situated in the world.

Before we start to examine the statutory residence test in a little more depth, I would like to briefly look at a tax case which was decided under the old rules which were in force prior to 6th April 2013 and which arrived at a very interesting conclusion. Under the old rules one would not expect be UK resident if you spent less than 183 days in the UK and less than 91 days on average over the last four years (see Appendix A for the old rules). These were well established rules which could be repeated a little like the multiplication tables older readers will be familiar with, and they were repeated equally by taxpayers and their advisers alike. A mantra if you will. 183 and 91. 183 and 91. What do you do if you want to be non-UK resident? Do not be in the country for more than 183 days in any particular tax year and more than 91 days on average over the last four years. This was very comforting to those chanting the mantra. It was therapeutic. The problem was that the Inland Revenue, now HM Revenue & Customs, never thought that it was that simple. There was a lot more to this than mere number crunching. How else could one explain their challenge to Dave Clark?

Mr Gaines-Cooper had moved to the Seychelles and lived there for 30 years. That is a very long time indeed. He relied on HM Revenue & Customs published guidance in a widely available booklet known as IR20 to maintain that he had left the UK and was non-resident. I remember that IR20 was around throughout much of my professional career. Mr Gaines-Cooper spent no more than 91 days in the UK in any particular tax year and so would have been within those rules. For number crunchers it was a clear cut issue. 183 and 91.

It was nevertheless found by the court that Mr Gaines-Cooper had not sufficiently severed his family ties in the UK; there was more to determining the quality of his residency than mere day counting. As a result it was found that he never really ceased being resident in the UK despite long absences, despite keeping his UK visits within the limits of the mantra and despite setting up home abroad.

The court found that England had remained, 'the centre of gravity of his life and interests'. It found that he had never cut his ties with Berkshire, where he grew up, and Oxfordshire, where the court ruled that his mansion, near Henley, continued to be his 'chief residence'.

Perhaps with an eye on the future Lord Justice Moses said that Mr Gaines-Cooper had failed to show 'a distinct break' from his social and family ties in the UK and that his complaints of unfair treatment were based on an 'impossible construction' of the law. The judge, sitting with Lord Justice Dyson and Lord Justice Ward, said that the 91 day rule could not establish non-residence status, but was 'important only to establish whether non-resident status, once acquired, has been lost'. Put another way, Mr Gaines-Cooper had never left the UK for tax purposes. Just think of the tax implications. It was not simply many years of tax and interest on unpaid tax which had potentially to be paid on the basis of the worldwide income of Mr Gaines-Cooper; it was also a problem in that tax returns had probably not been submitted for the years in question. An understandable omission since Mr Gaines-Cooper considered himself non-resident for those years and on very reasonable grounds … but if he had got it wrong there would also be penalties to consider.

I remember very well the shock amongst professional advisers as it became apparent that the number crunching mantra no longer reflected the certainties it once had for them. If one case demonstrates the 'adhesive' quality of UK residence this is the one!

Every tax case pre-dating the new rules which is mentioned in this book finds at the very least an echo in those new rules and that of Mr Gaines-Cooper is no exception. HM Revenue & Customs maintained that although he fell within the accepted number crunching rules of the time, the problem he had was that as far as the tax authorities were concerned he had never actually left the UK and that his visits to the country were of such a nature and quality that he had always been resident in the UK.

The statutory residence test gives much greater certainty regarding whether one is UK resident or not. However, while the current rules are certainly clearer; they are in many ways more restrictive and more demanding of the departing taxpayer. Like Mr Gaines-Cooper there will be many who genuinely believe that they have left the UK on a particular day and have not been resident for any subsequent tax year. The statutory residence test   is much more precise than the somewhat uncertain and arguably subjective position under the old rules though some may find that they too are still UK resident or may be deemed to have left at a date other than that they think they have or have inadvertently become UK resident for a year as a result of visits and circumstances.   All of these possibilities can have tax and reporting consequences.   In a nutshell, the statutory residence test favours those who keep good records and use their knowledge of the rules to inform their actions.

So, let us turn to the essence of the statutory residence test.

Chapter 2 – The Rules

The statutory residence test was introduced by HM Revenue & Customs on the 6th April 2013 to determine the residence status of individuals with connections to the UK. Ultimately, the purpose of the statutory residence test is to determine whether an individual is a resident in the UK for tax purposes.

The statutory residence test is therefore crucial for any individual leaving the UK and it is necessary to set out its fundamental tenets as a precursor to examining the temporary non-residence provisions since the test will determine when you have left and whether you remain resident or non-resident for subsequent years. It is not possible to consider temporary non-residence without viewing it through the lense of the statutory residence test. That is as it should be because the anti-avoidance rule is there to protect the interests of HM Revenue & Customs.

There are three essential components to the statutory residence test:

The automatic overseas test sets out factors which, if they are met, prove that a taxpayer is conclusively non-resident.

If the individual is not conclusively non-resident, it is then necessary to consider the automatic residence test, which sets out the factors which prove that someone is conclusively UK resident.

If neither the automatic overseas test or the automatic residence test is met, it is then necessary to establish whether a person has 'significant ties' with the UK so that they can be considered UK resident.

The Automatic Overseas Tests

You would normally be considered a non-UK resident by HM Revenue & Customs if you meet any one of the following three automatic overseas tests:

The First Automatic Overseas Test

You were UK resident in one or more of the three previous tax years preceding the year under consideration, but you spend or have spent fewer than 16 days in the UK in that tax year.

The Second Automatic Overseas Test

You were non-UK resident in each of the three tax years preceding the year under consideration and you spend or have spent fewer than 46 days in the UK in that tax year.

The Third Automatic Overseas Test

You work full-time outside the UK and spend fewer than 91 days in the UK and you work fewer than 31 days in the UK for three hours or less in any given day. Work abroad for these purposes is considered to be full-time if it is on average more than 35 hours a week over the whole tax year. Where some employment duties are performed in the UK one can spend up to 30 days a year in the UK without jeopardizing your non-resident status.

Straight away then one can see that outside of a work context and within certain limits the more time you spend non-UK resident the more days you can spend in the UK without compromising your position with respect to the automatic overseas tests. To qualify under the automatic overseas test outside of a work context it is advisable to keep return visits to the UK to no more than 16 days for the first three years but once it is certain that one has become non-resident for three years the relevant visits can be increased up to 46 days, almost a three-fold increase.

The Automatic Residence Tests

If the automatic overseas test is inconclusive, or you fail each of the components, that is not an end to the matter; the next step is to consider the automatic residence test.

If you meet any of these requirements you will be considered a UK resident.

The First Automatic Residence Test

You spend more than 183 days in the UK in the tax year. That is straightforward and follows previous guidance from HM Revenue & Customs (see Appendix A).

The Second Automatic Residence Test

You have a home in the UK during all or part of the tax year under consideration and you spend at least 30 days inside the tax year there (not necessarily consecutively) and during any 91 day period (of which 30 must be in the relevant tax year) you have no home overseas or if you do have an overseas home you spend no more than the permitted amount of time there (that is 30 days or less). A sufficient amount of time is presence in the UK home for at least 30 days in the tax year.

The Third Automatic Residence Test

You work in the UK for 365 days with no significant break.

The total number of working days is measured by any 365 day period where more than 75% of the days comprise more than three hours work in the UK.

Straight away one can see that spending over half a year in the UK or working full-time in the UK will render you automatically UK resident as will having available accommodation and spending 30 or more days there in most circumstances.

In connection with the second test involving the home, examples 4 to 8 in HM Revenue & Customs Guidance Note RDR3 on presence are useful for those looking to get to grips with the nitty gritty. I will also set out two examples to illustrate specific points in Chapter 3.

The Sufficient Ties Tests

The sufficient ties tests act as form of tie-breaker where neither the automatic overseas test nor the automatic residence test is conclusively met. It is here that we can sense the influence of the Gaines-Cooper case as well as that of the two cases reviewed towards the end of the book, amongst others.

The tests look at four or five relevant UK connections, called ties, and those ties are compared to the number of days that the individual spends in the UK in a tax year.

For an individual who was resident for one or more of the three tax years preceding the relevant tax year, the test operates as follows using four ties:

- Less than 16 days in the UK – non-resident.
- 16 to 45 days in the UK - only resident if at least 4 ties apply.

- 46 to 90 days in the UK - only resident if at least 3 ties apply.
- 91 to 120 days in the UK - only resident if at least 2 ties apply.
- 121 to 182 days in the UK - only resident if at least 1 tie applies.
- More than 183 days in the UK – always resident.

This information is summarized in tabular form in Table A of the RDR3 Guidance which can be found on page 29 of the Guidance Note.

For an individual who was resident in the UK for none of the 3 tax years preceding the relevant tax year, the test works as follows:

- 46 - 90 days in the UK – only resident if all 4 ties needed.
- 91 - 120 days in the UK – only resident if at least 3 ties apply.
- Over 120 days in the UK - only resident if at least 2 ties apply.

The same information is summarized in tabular form in Table B of RDR3 which can also be found on page 29 of the Guidance.

The sufficient ties test essentially looks at whether you have connections with the UK which would deem you to be a resident in the country. The longer you stay in the UK the less the number of ties which are needed to ensure that you are UK resident. That makes sense. Conversely, the less time you are in the UK the more ties are needed to capture your residence status as one of UK residence.

So what are these connections or ties?

The Family Tie

You have a UK family tie if you have a spouse, a civil partner, someone with whom you are living as a partner or a minor child and they are resident in the UK.

A minor child who is only resident in the UK because they are in full-time education in the UK will not be considered a connecting factor provided they spend fewer than 21 days in the UK outside term time. A half term holiday will count as term time for these purposes.

The Accommodation Tie

You have a UK accommodation tie if:

You have 'available accommodation' for a continuous period of at least 91 days in the tax year, ignoring any gaps of fewer than 16 days. You must actually use the accommodation for a day at least.

Available accommodation is widely defined and will include a home in the UK, someone else's home, a holiday home, a temporary retreat or similar' and could even include the use of a hotel if the same hotel is always used.

Reference should also be made to chapter 3 for more detail on the accommodation tie.

The Work Tie

You have a UK work tie if you spend at least 40 days working in the UK, where a working day is defined as three hours for these purposes.

The 90 Day Tie

You will have the 90 day tie if you spent more than 90 days in the UK in at least one of the previous two tax years.

The Country Tie

You will have the UK country tie if the UK is the country where the greatest number of days has been spent. In other words, if you have spent more days in the UK than in any other country during the tax year you will have a country tie. This tie applies only to those leaving the UK.

Understanding how many ties are required to determine your residence status will therefore depend on the number of days you spent in the UK during the tax year.

You should seek professional advice to arrive at an accurate assessment of the number of days spent in the UK in a tax year particularly where you believe that your UK days are close to one of the thresholds. Why is that?

You will need at the very least a second opinion on the time you have spent or are going to spend in the UK as a consequence of the complexities of the 'day counting' rules highlighted in the next chapter. Just when it was beginning to look as though everything is straightforward!

It is interesting to see how the sufficient ties test attempts to regularise the sorts of factors which were pertinent in the Gaines-Cooper decision for each and every relevant tax year. Even so, elements of the sufficient ties tests inevitably remain fairly subjective and one can reasonably anticipate that that the attention of HM Revenue & Customs will tend to focus on those needing to grapple with these tests over the years to come. Residence status should become a fertile ground for enquiries by HM Revenue & Customs.

It is obviously preferable to fall squarely within the terms of either the automatic overseas test or the automatic residence test because these are fairly objective tests which carry relatively high degrees of certainty. Once one is looking at the sufficient ties test these are inevitably somewhat more subjective and reflect the uncertainties which have always existed for people who visit the UK intermittently or for significant periods.

Chapter 3 – Some Practicalities

As I said in the introduction, the enthusiasm of HM Revenue & Customs for maintaining that individuals remain UK resident despite spending most of their time overseas has not changed or diminished. That is clear looking through the statutory residence test and in particular the various ties which can bind people to the UK as set out in the sufficient ties test.

HM Revenue & Customs will always be skeptical of those who go overseas but are vague on when they actually left the UK, who go overseas but come back and those who go overseas but are constantly drawn back by things they own or activities they enjoy in the UK.

Oh, yes, that is most people then.

This chapter briefly considers some of the practical considerations which underlie the three tests.

Calculating Time Spent in the UK

If you spent more than 183 days in the UK in a given tax year, you would normally be considered a UK resident. That seems as clear as it was under the old rules set out in Appendix A. However, calculating the number of days spent in the UK is not necessarily straight forward as you may think.

HM Revenue & Customs have (helpfully?) set out a number of criteria for determining whether you have spent a day in the UK. The general rule is a good and practical one in that you are considered to have spent a day in the UK if you are here at midnight on any given day. Simple? In one sense very simple but it is not as quite simple as counting all the days you are present in the UK at midnight.

This general rule is also subject to three other factors: The deeming factor; the transit day factor; the exceptional circumstances factor.

Factor 1 Deeming

The deeming rule takes into consideration whether you have been UK resident in one or more of the previous three tax years, have three UK ties for the tax year or have been present in the UK for more than 30 days without being present at the end of each day.

The deeming rule will automatically change the number of days you spent in the UK, even if you were not present at the end of the day.

The concern of the Government in introducing the deeming rule was that the midnight test could be abused by individuals who spend large numbers of days in the UK without being present at midnight. Accordingly, it introduced a rule which applies to certain individuals who, on more than 30 days in a tax year, are present in the UK at some point but not at midnight. In such cases, all days in excess of the 30 day threshold on which such an individual is present in the UK at some point in the day will be included as days spent in the UK for the purposes of the day count.

The 'deeming rule' only applies to an individual who has at least three UK ties for a tax year and has been resident in the UK for at least one of the three tax years preceding the relevant tax year. The rule does not apply for the purposes of the third automatic overseas test, nor to determine whether an individual satisfies the 90 day tie or country tie.

For those wishing to consider the 'deeming rule' in greater depth I would recommend examples 14 and 16 in the RDR3 Guidance.

Factor 2 Transit

Transit days are not typically considered full days under the statutory residence test.

A transit day is a day where you entered the UK from another country en route to a further country. To be considered a transit day you must not have conducted any other business during your time in the UK and you should leave the day after you arrive. Any other business could potentially include conducting a meeting or meeting up with friends. However, simply having breakfast or dinner would probably be considered as part of your transit. How reasonable is that?

You should therefore seek clarity and transparency regarding your activities during your time in the UK as they could have an impact on your total days spent in the UK.

For those wishing to consider the 'transit rule' in greater depth I recommend examples 17 and 18 a, b, c in the RDR3 Guidance which also gives some useful pointers as to how the transit rule interacts with the deeming rule.

Factor 3 Exceptional Circumstances

The legislation also provides for exceptional circumstances; these are circumstances where an individual spends a day in the UK for reasons beyond their control, such as national or local emergencies, for example war, civil unrest or natural disasters or sudden or life threatening illness or injury. This provision is restricted to a maximum of 60 days in any tax year. That is quite a generous limit but you will need to negotiate your particular circumstances with HM Revenue & Customs and you should be willing and capable of providing the fullest documentary evidence subject to circumstances. As I have already said in a different context, assume nothing. The mindset of HM Revenue & Customs can be summed up in one phrase, "Prove it". It is not an unreasonable mindset and in a later chapter we will see the cost of being unable or unwilling to 'prove it'.

So if you are in the UK due to exceptional circumstances, for instance a family bereavement, you may be granted special conditions with regards to the total number of days you have spent in the UK.

Split Years

The idea of split years is something which is absolutely fundamental to understanding your position under the statutory residence test and temporary non-residence provisions. The statutory residence test is based on a consideration of tax years. Split year treatment essentially means, however, that you will be deemed to have left the UK part way through a tax year rather than by reference to UK tax years ended 5th April.

Before Finance Act 2013 taking advantage of split years was only given on a concessionary basis as you will see in Appendix A. The concession was exactly that and any suspected or alleged abuse would have allowed HM Revenue & Customs to withdraw it at their discretion. What HM Revenue & Customs considered to be abuse was always a grey area and so presented a powerful tool which could be used to rule out of court anything which might be rightly or wrongly construed as controversial by HM Revenue & Customs. That is no longer possible. The fact that the tax year can now be split without relying on a concession gives far greater certainty, in many cases, over the date on which someone has left for tax purposes…and that is a very good thing.

It should never, however, be assumed that the year can always be split because the opportunities to do so on leaving the UK are very strictly limited to where the individual or their partner are starting full-time work overseas, or where an individual ceases to have a home in the UK.   Retired couples who move overseas for instance, but retain a home in the UK, are unlikely to be able to split the year on departure.

Let us quickly look at the three cases in a little more detail.

Case 1 – You were UK resident during the previous tax year to the one under consideration, are non-resident for the following year because you meet the third automatic overseas test, work on average 35 hours a week overseas without a significant break and keep days in the UK within permitted limits over a period to the end of the year.

For those wishing to consider case 1 in greater depth I recommend example 34 in the RDR3 Guidance.

Case 2 – You were UK resident for the previous tax year to the one under consideration, non-resident for the following year and have a partner who falls within case 1 for the relevant tax year or the previous tax year and you have left the UK to join that partner so that you can continue to live together while the partner is working overseas. After departure, you must either have no UK home or, if you have homes in both the UK and overseas, must spend the greater part of the time living in the overseas home.

For those wishing to consider case 2 in greater depth I recommend examples 35 and 36 in the RDR3 Guidance.

Case 3 – You were UK resident for the previous tax year to the one under consideration, are non-resident for the following tax year, and at the start of the tax year had at least one home in the UK but at some point in that year you cease to have any UK home and this continues until the end of that year.

The importance of the leaving rules in the context of split years is that which case you fall within will determine the date from which you are regarded as not resident in the UK and this will in turn impact on just how long you have been non-UK resident and the precise application of the temporary non-residence provisions, if appropriate.

There is an order of priority.

For someone leaving the UK, case 1 has priority over case 2 and case 3; case 2 has priority over case 3.

If you do not fall within any of the above three cases then you will not be entitled to the split year treatment.

A Word on 'Home' and 'Accommodation'

For most of us the concepts of 'home' and 'accommodation' are pretty much interchangeable, after all, home is what one tends to call the accommodation one lives in.

For our purposes however they are not quite the same thing at all.

'Home' is a term which applies to the second automatic residence test while 'accommodation' is a term of relevance to one of the five sufficient ties tests. It can be easy to mix them up. For the statutory residence test we are literally looking at a home but for the tie we are merely looking at 'available accommodation'. The latter is more transient and does not imply the same stability or permanence as a home.

Home and the Automatic Residence Test

There are two main questions to address.

The first is, 'so what is a home?'

A home can be a building (or part of a building), a vehicle, vessel or structure of any kind which is used as a home by an individual. It will be somewhere which an individual uses with a sufficient degree of permanence or stability to count as a home. This is very much in line with the capital gains tax legislation for an individual's main residence, of course.

A place can still be a home even if an individual does not stay there continuously. If, for example they move out temporarily but their spouse and children continue to live there, then it is still likely to be their home.

 If an individual moves out of their home completely and makes it available to let commercially on a permanent basis it will not be their home during the period it is let unless they or their family retain a right to live there. This can happen, for example, where the rental agreement permits the individual to use the property or part of the property as living accommodation.

If an individual completely moves out of a property and makes no further use of it whatsoever it will no longer be their home.

A building, vehicle, vessel or structure, or the like, can be an individual's home even if it is not owned by them. Whether ownership of a freehold or a tenancy makes no difference. For example a property that an individual rents or in which an individual lives with their parents, another member of their family or others will represent a home if they use it as their home.

If the individual has more than one home in the UK, the test must be applied to each home separately and not in aggregate. This means those with more than one home in the UK could spend time in a number of homes in succession and not be caught by this rule as any home in which the individual is present for less than 30 days in the tax year is ignored. Similarly, presence in any place which is not considered a 'home' is ignored.

There is a very interesting example in the RDR3 Guidance Note, example 9, which neatly illustrates the point that the 30 day limit is per house, not per individual.

Fatima has had four UK homes for several years. In the tax year under consideration, Fatima is present in her home in Swansea on 15 days, 20 days in her home in Loch Lomond, 29 in her London flat and 29 in her Newcastle flat. Fatima has been present on 91 days in total in those UK homes.

However, as she was not present in any individual home on at least 30 days, she will not have spent a sufficient amount of time in any single UK home. She will not meet the second automatic

UK test for the tax year under consideration. Rather interestingly, the legislation places a person with several homes in a better position than a person with one home if they understand the legislation and are prepared to act on it.

When considering whether you had a home in the UK or abroad HM Revenue & Customs may well seek to establish evidence firstly, as to whether a home existed and secondly to establish presence at a particular home. The sorts of evidence they may look at could include utility bills, lifestyle purchases, insurance, the address to which personal post, bank accounts, driving licenses are registered. It can even extend to things such as mobile phone usage and SORN notifications that a vehicle in the UK is 'off road'. Sound a bit like a formal enquiry?

The second question is, "So, if you have a home when does it become relevant for the second automatic residence test?"

You will meet the second automatic residence test if, in any 91 consecutive day period:

- You have a home in the UK and at least 30 of those days fall within the tax year under consideration and,

- You spend sufficient time there, sufficient being defined as at least 30 days and,

- You either have no overseas home or, if you do have an overseas home, you are present in it for 30 days or less in the tax year.

Example 8 in the RDR3 Guidance Note on presence is probably the best illustration of how this can work in practice. Although it refers to someone coming to the UK rather than someone leaving, it provides an extremely clear rendition of the rules.

Rosa is a professional cricketer who lives in New Zealand. She comes to the UK for the summer of 2015 to play for a UK team. She rents a house in Dorking for 4 months commencing 1st May 2015. She is present in her Dorking home on 100 days in 2015/2016. After the English cricket season ends she returns to New Zealand.

Throughout 2015/2016 Rosa owns a house in New Zealand. She is present in that house on 200 days in 2015/2016. While she is in the UK, Rosa lets out her New Zealand home on a commercial basis to a third party, from 1st June to 31st August 2015 (92 days). For that period the New Zealand house is not Rosa's home.

What is important here is that there is a period of 91 consecutive days (in fact a period of 100 days), at least 30 of which fall in the 2015/2016 tax year, when Rosa had a UK home where she spends a sufficient amount of time (i.e. at least 30 days), and when she does not have an overseas home (because it has been let out) in that period. Rosa consequently meets the second automatic UK test for 2015/2016.

If Rosa had not let out her New Zealand house and it had remained available for Rosa to use throughout the summer, it would have remained her home and Rosa would not have met the second automatic UK test.

Accommodation and the Sufficient Ties Test

Accommodation has a different meaning for the purpose of the sufficient ties test. Essentially the term refers to any accommodation which is available for you to use in the UK and which you do actually use.

Accommodation is regarded as available to you for a continuous period of 91 days if you are able to use it, or it is at your disposal, at all times throughout that period subject to the 16 day gap rule covered below. If a relative were to make their home available to you casually, for a social visit, say, it will not mean that the accommodation would be regarded as being available to you.

However, if it is available to you for a continuous period of 91 days and you do actually use it casually, it will be a tie.

Similarly, a casual offer from a friend to 'stay in my spare room any time' will not constitute an accommodation tie unless your friend really is prepared to put you up for 91 days at a time whether he actually does so or not. If there is a gap of fewer than 16 days between periods when accommodation is available the gap period is ignored and accommodation is regarded as being available throughout.

The rules change slightly if an individual stays at the home of a close relative. Close relative for these purposes means parent, grandparent, brother, sister and child or grandchild aged 18 or over (whether or not they are blood relatives, half-blood relatives or related by marriage or civil partnership). Child includes any adopted children. If an individual stays with a close relative the accommodation will be an accommodation tie if they spend at least 16 nights there in any one tax year and it is available to them for a continuous period of at least 91 days.

If an individual stays in UK accommodation held by a spouse, partner or minor children then they will be considered to have an accommodation tie if they spend at least a single night there.

Accommodation owned by an individual but which they have wholly let out commercially would not be considered as available to live in unless they retained the right to use the property or part of the property. Accommodation that is available to an individual but in which they have not spent at least one night in the tax year will not be an accommodation tie.

Short stays at hotels and guesthouses will not usually be considered to be an accommodation tie. However, if an individual books a room in the same hotel or guesthouse (and does not cancel those bookings) for at least 91 days continuously in a tax year, bearing in mind that short gaps may be discounted, it will be an accommodation tie.

A Word on 'Full-Time'

It should be noted that although the term 'full-time' has been removed from the test in Finance Act 2013 it is used in the guidance of HM Revenue & Customs and, since the aim is to determine whether the person works an average of 35 hours or more per week in the UK by applying a five step calculation (which is found in FA 2013, Sch 45, para 9(2) for those who are interested, this is most people's understanding of full-time. Any hours worked in the UK on days where more than three hours work is performed overseas are disregarded.

As noted above in connection with the working abroad test, the real difficulty with this 'sufficient hours' calculation is the absolutely astonishing amount of record keeping that is required on the part of the taxpayer. The guidance above regarding timesheets also applies to the working in the UK test. It is important to be aware that the working hours need to be assessed over "any given period of 365 days" and this test is assessed if any part of the 365 day period falls in the tax year (even if this is only one day). On this basis, the taxpayer will need to continually assess this every day until the test is satisfied. At the point the test is satisfied, it can be ignored for the rest of the tax year. The test needs to be reassessed at the start of the next tax year, at which point the review cycle begins again.

This demonstrates a fundamental law of the tax universe – if something can be made complex rather than simple then there is an irresistible force which will make it so. Just accept it!

A full 8 pages of RDR3 are devoted to explaining this concept of 'full-time'!

Conclusion

Problems are likely to arise in applying the statutory residence test where, not uncommonly, people to go overseas, spend most of their time there and assume that they are not UK resident. They will either not have completed forms SA109 or a P85 (see Appendix C for an explanation of these forms) because there is no obligation to and their records of the days of departure from and arrival in two or more countries and the quality of time they spend in particular locations and particularly the UK are patchy. They then spend quite a few days in the UK, often for very good reasons, and so fail the automatic overseas test and find themselves struggling with the second automatic residence test or the number of ties they have.

So, would Dave Clark have been non-resident under the current statutory residence test?

The answer is an emphatic 'Yes'. He would have clearly satisfied the first automatic overseas test. He was UK resident in one or more of the previous three tax years, and he spent fewer than 16 days in the UK in the relevant tax year. In fact, he spent no time in the UK at all during the relevant tax year. What a good idea that was!

There is, however, a catch. That catch is what this book is all about.

The next question would be whether he was temporarily non-resident?

We are not talking here about a general understanding of whether you are non-UK resident on a temporary basis. Undoubtedly, Dave Clark would be non-resident for a relatively short period which 'just happened' to cover an entire UK tax year. That is not the same thing at all as being 'temporarily non-resident'.

We now move seamlessly into the subject matter of this book: temporary non-residence, the anti-avoidance provision of the statutory residence test.

SECTION 2 – THE TEMPORARY NON-RESIDENCE PROVISIONS

Chapter 4 – Why?

Whether or not the split year provisions apply in any particular case, people are generally now much more likely to know whether they may be considered UK tax resident or not for a particular tax year. As the statutory test operates separately in relation to each tax year it is possible for an individual to be non-UK resident for one or a limited number of tax years even if UK resident both before and after. This can be especially important where residence status changes.

In the past, if someone claimed to have been non-UK resident for just a single tax year, within a period of UK residence either side, it is likely that, if challenged by HM Revenue & Customs, it would be on the grounds that they had remained UK resident throughout. Have a look at Appendix A on the old rules and you will see that it might be very difficult to convince HM Revenue & Customs that you had ever left the UK. Dave Clark was able to succeed where many others have failed because of his special and specific circumstances and an extremely good plan.

Since it is arguably much easier to become non-UK resident following Finance Act 2013, the statutory test for non-residence includes a general anti-avoidance rule to counteract the potential tax advantages which might otherwise be achieved should an individual be non-UK resident for a short period only.

Without the anti-avoidance rule it would be relatively easy for an individual to arrange to be non-resident for a year or so and in that period of non-residence arrange to receive certain income or dispose of assets free of UK tax. To be a short term tax exile would be a very attractive proposition for some.

While becoming a tax exile for a year is well established in popular legend, I do not believe that anyone has ever taken it to the extremes of the fictional keyboard player of plutonium rock band Disaster Area, Hotblack Desiato. Hotblack appears in a cameo role in Douglas Adams, 'The Restaurant at the End of the Universe'. He is, regrettably, unable to talk with the character Ford Prefect because "he is spending a year dead for tax reasons." With apologies to London based readers, yes, Hotblack Desiato is an estate agency and, yes, the estate agency did precede the naming of the fictional musician.

While there is no concept of, and certainly no possibility of, spending a single year dead for tax purposes in UK tax law, the closest equivalent in the real world is to spend a whole tax year non-UK resident and we have seen through Dave Clark how this might be achieved. Another spooky coincidence – In 1978 Pink Floyd, reputedly the inspiration for Disaster Area, spent an entire year outside the UK. They were not alone, of course.

While I find it hard to believe that Hotblack Desiato was the inspiration for the temporary non-residence provisions, I am sure that cases successfully exploiting non-UK residence for relatively short periods of time to mitigate tax liabilities played its part in envisaging and implementing the new legislation. Indeed, an Inspector of Taxes who was around in the 1970's might quip, 'Won't get fooled again'!

The anti-avoidance rule is clearly designed to prevent people from becoming non-UK resident for a relatively short period of time and, during this time, crystallising or receiving substantial income or capital gains which are not taxable in the UK due to the person's residency status.

The targets of the anti-avoidance rule are consequently sources where the timing of receipts can be determined by the emigrating person for capital gains and certain sources of income which have effectively been accumulated prior to leaving the UK. Such UK tax avoidance is prevented by identifying the income and gains and then taxing these sources in the tax year in which the person returns to the UK. That is the anti-avoidance rule in a nutshell. Interestingly, the anti-avoidance rule occupies a mere nine pages of the 109 page RDR3 Guidance ... which is out of all proportion to its importance.

The sort of scenario which the legislation is designed to combat is best illustrated through a simple example. Suppose Ben left the UK for a couple of tax years and decided to visit the UK during that couple of years for no more than two weeks in either year such that he would qualify as non-resident under the first automatic overseas residence test. Ben has an investment asset, an investment property, standing at a £100,000 gain which could, after allowing for the annual exemption, be taxed at rates of between 18% - 28%. In other words the tax at stake would be between £16,000 and £25,000. Merely by living outside the UK for a couple of years would result in a significant tax saving for Ben. Similar opportunities might also be achievable where Ben could receive the proceeds of, say, a life policy or a dividend from a company which he controlled while non-UK resident.

Following the March 2016 Budget, the tax rates on many investment assets fell to 10% - 20% and the accompanying liability in Ben's example to between £10,000 - £20,000 respectively where the investment asset is other than residential property. Residential property continues to be taxed at the 18% or 28% rates as appropriate, as is the case with Ben.

If Ben were abroad indefinitely then that result is perfectly achievable (subject to another more recent anti-avoidance provision now found in TCGA 1992 s 14B of which more later) but the anti-avoidance rule effectively maintains that to achieve that objective one would need to be non-resident for several years which may be simply too onerous for those who have a shorter term perspective. Ben was thinking more in terms of living abroad for a year on what amounts to an extended holiday to save £25,000 in tax. It would fund his sabbatical and there would be some left over on his return. That would be one thing but living abroad for, say, 6 years to achieve the same result was not really what Ben had in mind. That is not an extended holiday by any stretch of the imagination unless one was overseas for non-tax reasons....hence the rule.

The rule also prevents non-UK domiciled remittance basis users from remitting pre-departure income and gains tax-free during short periods of non-UK residence. Where a remittance basis user becomes UK resident after a period of temporary non-residence, the individual may be taxed on certain income and gains received or remitted to the UK arising in the period of temporary non-residence.

The new temporary non-residence rules only apply if your year of departure is 2013/2014 or later.

Chapter 5 – How?

The purpose of the temporary non-residence rule is now transparent. While you will be regarded as non-resident for tax purposes where you meet the relevant statutory residence test you can still in principle be taxed on capital gains or on certain types of income accruing prior to departure for several years.

The concepts surrounding residency have always been challenging. There are some who say that they are on a par to those found in theoretical or mathematical physics.

Really?

Well, consider this statement by HM Revenue & Customs which comes directly from the RDR3 Guidance Note:

"Note that the year of departure may fall earlier than the year in which you physically leave the UK."

Could this be the time to re-read the Hitchhikers Guide to the Universe?

I will do my best to explain how you could be temporarily non-resident when in reality you are not only genuinely resident in the UK under the statutory residence test but have also not even left the country. Hopefully, this will become crystal clear in the intriguingly titled chapter 'Mad Max' but we need to look at anti-avoidance rule in a little more depth before we meet Max.

A few idea's unique to temporary non-residence need to be considered, clarified and defined first; namely 'sole UK residence', 'residence period' and the 'rule of four of seven'. These three ideas really define what is meant by temporary non-residence so please bear with me and I will attempt to make the explanation as painless as possible.

What Does Sole UK Residence Mean?

Sole UK residence is a term which specifically applies to the idea of temporary non-residence. As always, it is important to distinguish between circumstances where the split year treatment applies and where it does not.

You will have sole UK residence for a residence period consisting of an entire tax year ended 5th April if you are resident in the UK for that year, and there is no time in that year when you are treaty non-resident.

Translation: If you are UK resident under the statutory residence test and are not resident elsewhere under a double tax treaty then that year will be a tax year of sole UK residence. If you are UK resident under the statutory residence test and are also resident elsewhere under a double tax treaty then that year will not be a tax year of sole UK residence.

You will have sole UK residence for a residence period consisting of part of a split year if the residence period is the UK part of that year and there is no time in that part of the year when you are treaty non-resident.

Translation: If you are entitled to split year treatment and you are UK resident under the statutory residence test and are not resident elsewhere under a double tax treaty then that period will be a period of sole UK residence. If you are entitled to split year treatment and you are UK resident under the statutory residence test and are resident elsewhere under a double tax treaty then that period will not be a period of sole UK residence.

It is worth noting as an aside that the definition of temporarily non-resident is slightly opaque because it is designed to achieve two separate objectives. While the overall thrust is to subject individuals to income tax in certain circumstances and capital gains tax generally where they are nevertheless non-UK resident under the statutory residence test, it attempts to do this in two distinctly separate circumstances: Where the individual is non-UK resident under the statutory test and where the individual is non-UK resident under the tie-breaker clause in a double tax treaty. The main consequence of the latter is that the anti-avoidance rule overrides double tax treaties in certain cases where a treaty might otherwise dis-apply UK legislation for an individual who remains UK resident under UK domestic law.

What Does Residence Period Mean?

The definition of temporary non-residence is expressed in terms of residence periods and operates where an individual is temporarily non-resident.

This is important because an individual is temporarily non-resident if, following a UK residence period; he or she is non-UK resident for a period of five years or less.

Again, residence period is a term which specifically applies to temporary non-residence and it is important to distinguish between circumstances where the split year treatment applies and where it does not.

In relation to whether you are temporarily non-resident, a residence period is either:

A full tax year beginning 6th April and ending on the following 5th April if you are not entitled to the split year treatment or

The overseas part of a split year or the UK part of a split year where you are entitled to the split year treatment.

The Rule of Four of Seven

Before the concepts of 'sole UK residence' and 'residence period' can be applied to your circumstances it is necessary to ensure that a third and very specific rule is satisfied – what I call the rule of four of seven which is alluded to above. It is not an official term like the other two but the phrase has the virtue of telling it like it is.

For the anti-avoidance rule to apply, you must have been UK resident in at least four of the seven tax years prior to the year in which non-residence commences. The rule of four of seven is straightforward provided you are able to ascertain your position for the last seven years under the statutory residence test. This is why you need to have a grasp of your residence status for the seven years preceding your departure from the UK as part of a twelve year mindset.

On general principles, then, a period of temporary non-residence starts from the date following that on which the last residence period for which you had sole UK residence ends. Turn it over in your mind. It makes sense.

If you are not entitled to the split year treatment then you are looking at whole UK tax years. In these circumstances the date immediately following the last residence period in which you were solely resident in the UK (referred to as Period A) would represent the commencement of your temporary non-residence. i.e. Period A would be the last complete tax year for which you were wholly UK resident.

Where you are entitled to the split year treatment the period of temporary non-residence starts on the day after the date of the end of the last residence period for which you have sole UK residence.

What?

Sole UK Residence, Residence Period and the rule of four of seven are best understood by way of example.

Let us quickly look at three examples with the one purpose of illustrating how this works in practice. It should become clear.

David & Split Years

David had sole UK residence for the previous seven tax years (referred to as "period A" in the RDR3 Guidance). He leaves the UK indefinitely on 6th October 2015 and is entitled to the split year treatment. David's period of non-residence commences on 6th October 2015. Blisteringly obvious? Yes, of course, but consider his friend George who is in exactly the same position. The facts are identical but for just one difference.

That one difference is that George is not entitled to the split year treatment.

George & Tax Years

Period A, George's last tax year of sole UK residence, would finish at the end of the tax year ended 5th April 2015, i.e. 2014/2015 and his period of temporary non-residence would consequently start on 6th April 2015, even though he did not physically leave the UK until 6th October 2015.

Remember that slightly mysterious quote from HM Revenue & Customs: "Note that the year of departure may fall earlier than the year in which you physically leave the UK."

Ah ha.

The quote actually refers to a slightly different context but it nevertheless makes sense in this one.

Luther & the Rule of Four of Seven

Luther was resident in the Russian Federation for five out of the seven years to 5 April 2016 and was UK resident for the other two years. He then became non-resident again from that date. Luther expects to be non-resident until 5th April 2019 when he plans to return to the UK indefinitely. You might think that this is a straightforward case of temporary non-residence but it is not for Luther because of the rule of four of seven.

Luther was only resident in the UK for two years out of the last seven (2014/2015 and 2015/2016).

An individual is a temporarily non-resident for a period if both the period of non-residence is less than five years; and the individual was UK resident for at least four of the seven years preceding the year of departure.

Luther left the UK on 6th April 2016 (i.e. in 2016/2017) but he was resident for only two of the seven tax years preceding it. Although Luther expects to be non-resident for only three years, he does not meet the definition of temporary non-resident because he does not satisfy the rule of four of seven.

The anti-avoidance rule does not apply to Luther.

A Threat and an Opportunity

Since the statutory test imports the split year cases, the pertinent period runs for such cases five calendar years from the date of departure, in other words five complete years. When considering circumstances which qualify for split year treatment it is important to determine which case takes precedence on departure and return.

When considering circumstances which do not qualify for split year treatment it is crucial to ensure that you are absolutely clear on when your period of non-residence commences for the purposes of the anti-avoidance rule and to give due consideration to whether you are likely to qualify for split year treatment on your return (see Chapter 17).

It is inevitable that individuals who do not enjoy the split year treatment must remain non-UK resident for over five complete years to avoid the anti-avoidance rule. This requirement is sometimes known as the 'six year trap'.

As we have already seen, the second objective the anti-avoidance rule attempts to achieve is to subject individuals to income tax and capital gains tax where they are treated as non-resident for the purposes of a double tax treaty under the tie-breaker clause in the relevant treaty. You will consequently need to consider the relevant articles of any double tax treaty, where appropriate, which may exist between the UK and the country you are to become resident in.

With respect to treaty non-residence periods these are included in computing the period in which the individual is temporarily non-resident and as such this may give rise to a planning opportunity. The anti-avoidance rule can potentially be dis-applied in certain cases where an individual is non-resident under the statutory test for five or fewer tax years. Such cases are those where, before or after the period of non-residence, the individual is nevertheless treaty non-resident and inclusion of the treaty non-residence period causes the five year limit to be compromised.

The interaction of the 3 provisions is best illustrated by an example and I will use an annotated and extended version of one of HM Revenue & Customs own, example 42. It combines many of the earlier points. Consequently, if you understand Mad Max you will understand temporary non-residence.

Chapter 6 – Mad Max

Max has had sole residence in the UK for the previous 10 years to the one under consideration. That means that he was resident in the UK for those years and there was no time in those years when he was treaty non-resident. The latest complete tax year in which these conditions applied was 2013/2014. i.e., the year ended 5th April 2014.

Let us assume that Max is considering his status for the year ended 5th April 2015 (i.e. 2014/2015). For the purpose of this example, Max does not satisfy the conditions for split year treatment in tax year 2014/2015.

Just over 10 months into the 2014/2015 tax year Max leaves the UK. On 22nd February 2015 Max moves to Poland and is considered resident there from this point.

What are the effects?

Max retains his UK residence under the statutory residence test up to the end of the tax year ended 5th April 2015. Why? Because he cannot meet any of the automatic overseas tests. He meets the first automatic residence test and is not entitled to the split year treatment.

From 6th April 2015 he is resident in Poland for purposes of the statutory residence test.

From 22nd February to 5th April 2015 Max is also treaty non-resident under the UK/Poland double tax treaty. He is therefore effectively dual resident under the tax treaty.

Max cannot be solely UK resident from 22nd February 2015 for the purposes of the anti-avoidance rule. Why? Because although he is treated as UK resident for 2014/2015 under the statutory residence test he is also treaty non-resident for part of the tax year.

So what is the position in terms of temporary non-residence anti-avoidance rule?

Period A, the last tax year for which Max has sole UK residence for the purposes of the anti-avoidance rule will end at the end of the tax year 2013/2014, i.e. 5th April 2014, because that is the end of the last tax year in which Max was solely UK resident and he is not entitled to the split year treatment. His date of departure for the purpose of applying the temporary non-resident provisions is therefore 6th April 2014, even though he actually physically left the UK on 22nd February 2015 and even though he is regarded as UK resident for the whole tax year to 5th April 2015.

The next residence period begins on 6th April 2014 and Max will begin to be regarded as temporarily non-resident from this point. Note this is not the same as his UK resident status under the statutory residence test; it is for the purposes of the anti-avoidance rule.

Max returns to the UK on 26th May 2018 and split year treatment applies. Max has sole UK residence from 26th May 2018. He is treaty resident for the UK part of the year. His temporary non-residence ends on 25th May 2018. The period of temporary non-residence is therefore 6th April 2014 to 25th May 2018 inclusive, just over four years, which is less than five years and so Max is within the scope of the temporary non-residence provisions.

Max thought that he had left the UK on 22nd February 2015 and clearly this was the case as he remembers the day of his UK departure and arrival in Poland vividly. His airline ticket and other documentation confirm this. It was an important day in his life. However, for tax purposes he remained UK resident until the next 5th April and yet was deemed to have left a year earlier than that for purposes of the anti-avoidance rule. At the time of the start of his first new UK tax year in Poland he has already one year behind him in the context of the anti-avoidance rule.

If Max was not mad as he left for Poland he certainly was on his return. He inadvertently cashed in a life policy while in Poland thinking that it would not need to be declared to HM Revenue & Customs. Why should it, he thought? I am resident in Poland not the UK. The big consolation however is that his UK adviser picked it up and included an appropriate entry on his 2018/2019 self assessment tax return. There would be no compliance issue for Max.

Our thoughts might once again drift back to Albert Einstein who once quipped in a rare moment of frustration, "The hardest thing in the world to understand is the income tax. This is too difficult for a mathematician. It takes a philosopher."

However, had Einstein followed the story so far, he would have grasped concepts like sole residence, residence period and the rule of four of seven. He would also have grasped the idea of how tax years can inform the date on which you depart and how entitlement to split year treatment can alter that date. He might also have reflected that the split year basis is exactly how most people perceive non-residence since that is the way it appears to them and that the way it actually operates. It is commonsense. Looking at sole residence and residence periods might equate more to his own counterintuitive theories than to commonsense. The workings of the anti-avoidance rule is not really any more obvious than the fact that the earth is not flat. Observation alone will not lead you to understanding.

Although it may not be the easiest thing in the world to understand it is also not the hardest by a long way!

Max is a great example because it shows just how strange it can be.

To recap, Max physically left the UK on 22nd February 2015. Nevertheless:

His UK residence status under the statutory residence test is that he is UK resident until 5th April 2015 even though he left the UK on 22nd February 2015. He is therefore UK resident for the whole 2014/2015 tax year.

His temporary non-residence status is that he is not solely UK resident 22nd February 2015-5th April 2015 because he is also treaty non-resident. The last year he was solely UK resident was therefore 2013/2014 or the year ended 5th April 2014. Therefore Max is regarded as temporarily non-UK resident from 6th April 2014 even though he left the UK on 22nd February 2015.

Max is also a good example for considering whether the new rules apply to you in principle or whether they do not.

Earlier in this book I mentioned that the rules only apply from 2013/2014 onwards. In other words from 6th April 2013. Given everything that has been said so far it is perhaps confusing as to which year one might be said to have departed in order to determine which rules apply – the old ones or those starting with the 2013/2014 tax year. Fortunately, HM Revenue & Customs have provided some useful clarification.

The temporary non-residence provisions are only relevant where your year of departure, as uniquely defined in the RDR3 Guidance, is 2013/2014 or later. In the words of HM Revenue & Customs, "The new temporary non-residence rules only apply if your year of departure (as defined here) is 2013/2014 or later."

Fair enough but how do you determine that year for the purposes of the anti-avoidance rule?

Your year of departure is uniquely defined as the tax year including the last residence period for which you were solely resident in the UK or the date following that in which the last sole residence period ends. Whether this is unnecessarily complicated I leave to the reader to debate with him or her self. The reality is that HM Revenue & Customs needed some way of deciding which cases fell under the new rules and which would fall within the old rules.... and this is it.

So in HM Revenue & Customs example 42 in the RDR3 Guidance, Max leaves the UK on 22nd February 2015 and so, again in the words of HM Revenue & Customs, "his year of departure for the purpose of applying the temporary non-residence provisions is 2013/2014."

Why?

Because 2013/2014 was his last period of sole UK residence as we have already established. The new anti-avoidance rules therefore have to be considered.

If you have yet to depart the UK, or have only recently done so, you do not need to be concerned as to whether the anti-avoidance provisions could potentially apply to you. They do. If, however, you departed these shores any time around the cusp of the transition from the old to the new rules or before that cusp then you will need to consider when your deemed 'year of departure' was for these purposes.

If you understand Mad Max then you understand temporary non-residence!

But what exactly are the implications of being temporarily non-resident?

Chapter 7 – The Main Implications

Dave Clark was found to be non-resident back in the late 1970's.

We also concluded that this would also have been the case under the statutory residence test.

However, under temporary non-residence it looks as though he is in a similar position to Ben and Mad Max. Both satisfy the rule of four of seven. Both are non-resident for less than five years. Dave Clark would potentially have been caught by the anti-avoidance rule had he tried his planning today.

This, however, is where considering what would have happened becomes less informative.

The type of income which Dave Clark received is not of a type which, assuming one is caught by the rules, HM Revenue & Customs is particularly concerned about. That is fundamentally because the rules on how that type of income is taxed have changed since the 1970's.

Anyone who is self employed will appreciate that their tax liability for any given year is based on their tax adjusted profits for the accounting year ended in the relevant tax year. For instance, the tax year for 2015/2016, i.e. the year to 5th April 2016, would be based on the accounts to, say, 31st March 2016 or whatever accounting year ends in the tax year. That treatment, however, has only been the case from 1997/1998. Prior to that, the self employed were assessed on what was known as the prior year basis. In this example the tax adjusted profit for the year ended 31st March 2016 would have formed the basis not for 2015/16 but 2016/2017. While the rules back in the 1970's could be successfully managed in the way which Dave Clark did, it would be far more difficult to plan in a similar way today. So it does not matter at all that the type of income Dave Clark earned is not of a type caught by the anti-avoidance rule. It would be caught under general principles these days.

There are four main areas where individuals are likely to experience the effects of the anti- avoidance rule where they are resident overseas but, because they are not resident for more than five years and fall within the rule of four of seven, their receipts of capital gains or certain kinds of income during their non-residence nevertheless becomes liable to UK tax on their return to the UK.

These rules are therefore likely to impact on people who:

- Have significant chargeable assets for capital gains tax purposes (property, shares, investments, investment businesses) with large inherent gains which have accumulated by the time they leave the UK.

- Receive dividends or other distributions from their personal company or companies which can be identified with pre-departure profits.

- Are non-UK domiciled and have elected to use the remittance basis.

-   Are in receipt of certain other income which could be said to have accumulated prior to departure.

If you are potentially subject to the anti-avoidance rule the next step is to identify whether you have any potentially taxable receipts which are subject to UK tax while you are non-resident. I will look at these various exposed sources of income and capital in the next four chapters.

Chapter 8 – Capital Gains Tax

This is not a book on the minutiae of capital gains tax. Excellent accounts of the nature and scope of capital gains tax can be had from many sources and so I will give only the very briefest of overviews to set the scene.

Capital gains accrue to an individual, a UK resident, on the disposal of chargeable assets.

Chargeable assets for the purpose of capital gains tax include all forms of property wherever they are situated including shares and securities, interests in land, options, debts and rights over property, any currency other than sterling and any property which was created by the person disposing of it such as copyright or a lease. The definition of an asset in the capital gains tax legislation is extremely wide and includes incorporeal property generally. In this context, incorporeal property includes contractual rights, whether or not those rights are capable of being transferred or assigned, and whether or not they have a market value.

A disposal includes sale, gift or exchange of an asset in whole or in part.

Gains and losses on individual assets are worked out by deducting from the sale or market value in certain circumstances (for example, a gift) the original cost and incidental costs of acquisition, any expenditure which has increased the value of the asset and the incidental costs of disposal. An annual exemption is deducted from the gain (£11,100 2016/2017) and if the gain is below this amount there is no capital gains tax to pay.

Some assets can be disposed of without a capital gains charge. For instance private motor vehicles and an individual's only or main residence having gardens or grounds of half a hectare or less which has been occupied as such throughout the period of ownership and chattels.

Prior to 6th April 2016, if the gain were above this annual exemption it is taxed at 18% where the gains fall within the individual's otherwise unused basic rate income tax band and 28% thereafter.

All this changed following the Budget of March 2016.

A major theme of the March 2016 Budget was to differentiate between gains triggered on different categories of assets. The 10%, 18% and 28% rates remained and a new rate of 20% introduced but alongside some seismic shifts in who is to be taxed at which rate.

The March 2016 Budget reduced the higher rate of capital gains tax from 28% to 20%, with the basic rate falling from 18% to 10%, in relation to disposals made on or after 6th April 2016. The trust capital gains tax rate mirrored the personal higher rate reduction from 28% to 20%.

It has long been thought that the optimum rate of capital gains tax is around 18%; at that level people are inclined to regard it as more of an inconvenience rather than an obstacle in considering transactions which may be chargeable to capital gains tax. In other words it is considered that at 18% the number of transactions will increase when compared with the position where higher rates of capital gains tax are pertinent. The driver here therefore appears to have been to encourage investment and increase tax yields by making tax less of an issue in the context of decisions to sell investment assets. 10% is undoubtedly as good as it ever gets and no doubt some will believe that the Chancellor has gone too far in reducing the basic rate to this level.

However, amongst the types of property that do not qualify for the reduced capital gains tax rates is residential property.

Clearly, if you had chargeable assets which carried a significant gain within them one could in principle simply become non-resident for at least a year, dispose of the assets while non-resident and save 10%, 18%, 20% or 28% tax (subject to any taxes which applied in the jurisdiction in which you were resident, of course) …. unless it were for the anti-avoidance rule. That was Ben's plan.

The most important distinction between assets for the purposes of the temporary non-residence provisions is that between assets owned before departure from the UK and those which have been acquired afterwards.

In general terms, the legislation is targeted at the former rather than the latter.

Assets Owned Before Departure from the UK

Should an individual be non-resident under the statutory residence test and yet fall within the temporary non-resident rules, chargeable gains and allowable losses triggered in the period of absence are treated under section 10A of the Taxation of Chargeable Gains Act 1992 as accruing in the tax year during which the individual returns.

How does this work in practice?

Undoubtedly, this is best illustrated by a few examples.

Temporary Non-Residence and Sale in the Year of Return

Laura has been resident in the UK for many years. On 31st March 2015 she moved to Austria. Laura was not entitled to split year treatment. On 15th January 2020 she disposes of an asset that she had held before departure from the UK at a gain of £50,000. On 1st April 2020 she resumes UK residence.

Laura is treated as departing from the UK on 6th April 2015. She was non-resident under the statutory residence test for the whole of the four tax years, counting from the year after her departure: 2015/2016; 2016/2017; 2017/2018 and 2018/2019.

Laura returned to the UK before five complete tax years expired and, again, was not entitled to split year treatment. As a result she is treated as resident throughout the tax year of her return, 2019/2020.

The gain of £50,000 made in January 2020 is therefore chargeable in 2019/2020 UK tax year.

Temporary Non-Residence and Gains in an Intervening Year

Jonathan had lived all his life in the UK. He left the UK on 10th August 2014 for a three year contract of employment in New Zealand.

Jonathan resumed tax residence in the UK on 2nd September 2017.

He realised a chargeable gain on an asset acquired before he left the UK of £15,000 on 20th August 2015 while he was in New Zealand.

Jonathan meets the tests in TCGA 1992, s 10A:

- He was resident in the UK all his life before his departure, so he was resident in the UK at any time during each of at least four of the seven tax years immediately preceding his departure.
- He resumed UK residence before the expiry of five complete tax years.
- The asset sold in 2015 was one owned by him when he was resident in the UK, and not acquired subsequently.

Thus in the year of his return, 2017/2018, he is taxable on the gain of £15,000 made in the intervening year of 2015/2016.

Had Jonathan been entitled to the split year treatment on arrival and departure and spent at least 5 years outside of the UK, providing he continued to be employed in New Zealand, he would not have needed to report the gain or pay tax on it.

Gains and Losses

For the avoidance of doubt, as the gains are treated as accruing on a return to the UK the rate at which capital gains tax is charged is the rate applicable in the year of return rather than the rate applying in the UK tax year of disposal. If the tax rate had fallen in your absence and you had made a disposal that would be beneficial. If it had risen, it would not be beneficial. The changes to capital gains tax rates in the Budget of March 2016 may therefore have implications where a pre-departure asset has been or will be disposed of while you are non-resident but the temporary non-residence provisions apply.

Losses are allowed on same basis as gains are taxed. The computational rules, however, are those applicable in the UK tax year during the period of absence when the gains or losses were in fact triggered. Losses realised by those who are temporarily non-resident can be used to reduce gains of the same year which have come back into charge but cannot be carried forward. This could have significant consequences. Care should therefore be taken when making disposals in the early years of non-residence if a return to the UK within five years of departure is a possibility even if it is not specifically planned for.

For the avoidance of doubt the gains charged on return to the UK are the total gains triggered and not simply the part of each gain that was unrealised as at the commencement of the period of no-residence.

Assets Acquired After Departure from the UK

Gains triggered on assets acquired during the period of non-residence and disposed of while non-UK resident are in general excluded from UK tax, so where you are non-resident under the statutory residence test no gains on the disposal of those assets are taxable in the UK.

Predictably though this is not quite as simple as it may first appear.

How so?

This exclusion is itself subject to a number of exceptions, most notably for assets acquired under the holdover and rollover provisions.

These exceptions are not specifically identified in the RDR3 Guidance but you may find reference to them in both the legislation and in certain HM Revenue & Customs material. Useful reference may be made to HS278 which specifically refers to temporary non-residence and capital gains tax.

The exceptions relate to assets acquired after departure from the UK but under circumstances which nevertheless have a connection with the earlier period of residence. Gains accruing on the disposal of such assets during the intervening years are not excluded but are treated as chargeable in the tax year of return.

Rather than setting out in detail the nature of the vulnerable assets, reference should be made to gains accruing on the assets set out in Appendix B which remain within the scope of section 10A. I have included the statutory references for those whose circumstances may lead them to enquire further though you will need a copy of TCGA 1992 beside you, as amended.

To give a flavor of the type of circumstances you should be aware of HM Revenue & Customs provide a very useful example which I have annotated for purposes of illustration. Although it really deals with the position under the pre-statutory residence provisions, the principles nevertheless hold true for the exceptions under the current taxing regime. Comparable anti-avoidance rules were in force for the dates in this example.

Mr and Mrs Black have lived in the UK all of their lives. They departed the UK on 26th March 2010 for Mr Black to take up a contract of employment abroad. They resumed tax residence in the UK on 1st December 2013.

Mr Black had bought a chargeable asset in the UK on 14th September 2000. On 12th June 2011 he gave the property to Mrs Black. This transfer would not have given rise to a capital gains tax charge even if the couple had been UK resident because section 58 of TCGA 1992 applies to the gift such that for capital gains tax purposes at the time of transfer neither gain nor loss arises.

Mrs Black sells the property on 5th February 2012 realising a gain of £100,000. On the sale by Mrs Black, the gain is treated as accruing in the year of return as she fulfils all of the conditions for section 10A TCGA 1992 to apply, and the asset is not excluded from the scope of the section.

Without these provisions, Mrs. Black would have been able to sidestep paying any capital gains tax simply on the grounds that she acquired the asset while she was not resident in the UK. Too good to be true? It certainly is!

Furthermore, there will be issues with assets which have been subject to deferral reliefs. A gain or loss will not be excluded from the scope of section 10A if it represents a gain or loss on an asset which was held before the individual left the UK, and if that original gain or loss was 'held-over' or deferred so that it would not arise until another asset was disposed of. If that other asset is disposed of, crystallising the gain, while the individual is temporarily non-resident then the gain is not excluded from section 10A. Instead, the gain is treated as accruing in the year of return to UK tax residence.

It would have been too easy had that been the case.

There is no easy tax mitigation to be had by manipulating the above holdover, rollover and deferral reliefs!

The Old Rules

Previously, if an individual returned to the UK without having spent at least five complete tax years as a non-resident, gains realised in that period on assets that were held at the point of departure came back into charge upon return to the UK.

While this rule has been largely retained under the Finance Act 2013 provisions, the period is now five years from the date of departure in line with the statutory residence test and the temporary non-residence provisions, rather than five complete tax years. That is not the same thing, of course.

Do Not Forget All Those Other Rules

No changes were made to the principle that capital gains which have been held-over or rolled-over are clawed back if the recipient of the asset leaves the UK within 6 years after the end of the tax year of disposal. This is a very long standing anti-avoidance provision and essentially serves to charge the held-over or rolled-over gain where the recipient ceases to be resident in the UK in the six years after the tax year of the relevant disposal and while still holding the relevant asset.

The held-over gain generally becomes chargeable immediately before that time. There is a relaxation in this claw back rule where an individual works overseas. All the work duties must be performed outside the UK, and the individual must become resident in the UK again within three years, and while still holding the relevant asset.

To make matters worse, if the recipient does not pay the tax resulting from this claw back of relief within 12 months from the due date, HM Revenue & Customs can recover the tax from the donor instead, provided the tax is assessed no more than six years after the end of the tax year in which the relevant disposal took place.

Where anyone is going abroad they should therefore review any such transfers which have been made in the last six years.

Since the statutory residence test became law a further provision has been introduced which is not part of the test but which can nevertheless have profound consequences.

We have been looking at the temporary non-residence provisions which impose capital gains tax on assets which were purchased by an individual who was UK tax resident and subsequently sold after the owner had ceased to be UK resident. This only applies if the vendor returns to the UK within five years and is imposed in the tax year they return to the UK.

A second 'bite of the cherry' with respect to capital gains tax for HM Revenue & Customs is through section 14B TCGA 1992 which imposes capital gains tax on the disposal of UK residential properties by a non-UK resident.

Section 14B catches disposals of UK residential property by non-UK resident individuals, companies, partnerships or a personal representative of a non-resident deceased person. It overrides the overseas part of a split year for individuals. Property is therefore not only taxable at the highest rates of capital gains tax; it is also taxable whatever the residence status of the owner.

Happily, however, under s 14B, it is only the part of the gain which arises after 5th April 2015 is subject to tax.

The default method of calculating the gain is by reference to the property's market value at 5th April 2015, which becomes the base cost for capital gains tax purposes.   Alternatively, an irrevocable election can be made to time-apportion the gain over the entire period of ownership to determine the post-5th April 2015 gain.

The reporting obligation and the obligation to pay tax might be regarded by some as onerous.

A non-resident capital gains tax return is required irrespective of whether there is any chargeable gain. The return should reach HM Revenue & Customs within 30 days of conveyance (not exchange) of the property. HM Revenue & Customs can charge penalties for late filing of a return, which are the same as those applying for a self assessment return.

Any tax payable is also due within 30 days of the conveyance unless the taxpayer is in self assessment, when the normal payment date can apply instead, and the computation of the chargeable gain/allowable loss arising on the disposal should be included with the self assessment return.

Given the accelerated obligation to submit returns and settle the tax liability it may occur to some that it is probably better to dispose of UK residential property while UK resident and then report it under the self assessment regime than to dispose of the property while non- resident, whether temporarily non-resident or not.

Chapter 9 – Distributions From Your Personal Company

The majority of small companies, family companies and private companies are close companies, and so if a participator extracts any value from his or her company without income tax deduction there is likely to be a provision somewhere in the UK's tax rules which will impose either a corporation tax charge on the company or an income tax charge on the participator, or both.

There are now also the temporary non-residence rules to consider in appropriate circumstances. It would be just far too easy to arrange to receive a dividend from a close company while the owner was non-UK resident for a year without any tax implications.

Dividends and other distributions received from UK companies and from non-UK companies which would be close if they were UK resident during the period of absence are treated as received in the period of return where the temporary non-residence provisions apply. This boils down to the fact that if you have control over what amounts to a personal company and the company pays you dividends or makes distributions from pre-departure profits while you are temporarily non-resident those dividends are charged to UK tax when you return to the UK.

This dividend rule as I will call it is expressed as applying only to material participators in the company. As the term 'material' connotes ownership of 5% or more of the company very few close company participators are likely to fall outside of the provisions.

A few definitions will be really helpful here:

Broadly, a company is "close" if it is privately owned and controlled by five or fewer individual participators. That encompasses most companies which are owned by shareholder directors.

A participator is an individual who has a financial interest in the company. That interest could be in terms of voting power, ownership of the share capital of the company or ownership of rights to capital on winding up. A review of your company articles and shareholder agreement may be in order if there are any doubts on this score. Classic examples of participators include a shareholder, a director, or even a loan creditor.

In determining whether an individual is a participator or not one also needs to take into account any associates he or she may have.

An associate of a participator is defined as:

- Any 'relative'; the term 'relative' includes spouses, parents or remoter forebear, children or remoter issue, brothers or sisters (but not aunts, uncles, nephews and nieces). Separated spouses and half-brothers or sisters are associated. Divorced spouses and step-brothers or step-sisters are not associates.

- Any business partner.

- The trustee(s) of any settlement in which the participator (or any living or dead 'relatives') is or was the settlor; and the trustee(s) of a settlement or personal representatives of an estate holding company shares in which the participator has an interest (where the participator is a company, any other company interested in those shares is also an associate).

From 6th April 2016 the once familiar dividend tax credit is abolished and a dividend tax allowance introduced with differing tax rates depending on income levels above the threshold. That development now renders the temporary non-resident legislation even more pertinent. The rate of tax on dividend income above the £5,000 allowance is now 7.5% for basic rate payers, 32.5% for higher rate payers and 38.1% for additional rate taxpayers. Without the anti-avoidance rule this tax could be avoided on relatively short absences from the UK.

Furthermore, if significant dividends accumulate such that they are charged in a single tax year, the year of return to the UK, then it is worth calculating the potential tax impact as inadvertently bunching the payments for tax purposes in this way may easily render them taxable at the punitive rate of 38.1%.

Trading Companies

A limited exception to the general position that dividends may be taxed under the anti-avoidance provisions is made for trading companies insofar as the temporary non-residence rule does not apply to dividends paid in respect of post UK departure trading profits.

In the case of companies already in existence and trading, a 'just and reasonable' basis is used to allocate dividends between pre and post departure profits. It must be emphasised that this exception applies only to trading profits and therefore does not relieve any form of investment income. Again, the 'just and reasonable' basis is used to allocate a dividend as between trading income and investment income where the company has both.

Trading companies formed after departure are, not unreasonably, protected from the anti-avoidance rule because none of the profits relate to a period of UK residence.

Consequently, it is strongly advisable for the owners of trading companies to ensure that that their company records are capable of accurately identifying UK and overseas profits and of distinguishing between trading and investment income. If you are unable to do this you will struggle to take advantage of the exception.

For example, say Brett has a personal company which is incorporated in the UK. It is mainly a trading company but also holds a small property portfolio which generates rental income. Brett's records show that the company profits are derived 75% from its trading operations and 25% from its investment properties. If he were to become non-resident but also fell within the temporary non-resident provisions Brett's company records would need to be sufficiently accurate to enable him to separate trading from investment profit and to identify pre and post departure trading profit if he is to take proper advantage of the limited exception. That will also mean being able to properly apportion expenditure between trading and investment profits.

Lack of believable records coupled with vague assertions are likely to meet with, shall we say, interest from HM Revenue & Customs.

Groups of Companies

Many successful businesses start off as a single limited company. As a business grows its needs change and it may even diversify such that a group structure would have definite benefits; a number of companies form a group. A holding company will usually own the shares in its subsidiaries which may be trading or investment companies to a greater or lesser extent or, indeed, a mixture as is the case with Brett's single company.

A group structure may be beneficial for any number of reasons. Different companies may undertake very different activities and a holding company may become necessary to manage their diverse operations.

A holding company may also be useful to ring-fence valuable assets to protect them against potential claims. The assets that are usually ring-fenced are property and intellectual property.

Nevertheless, although this group structure may be convenient, practical and commercial, it may not be ideal where trading subsidiaries are held through a holding company and the shareholder in the holding company seeks to rely on the exception for trading companies.

Why?

The exception for trading profits does not, interestingly, appear to embrace group structures. Perhaps that is simply because of a perception that it is mainly 'singleton' companies which are likely to consider paying dividends while a participator is non-resident but I cannot see any obvious reason for this omission.

It follows that dividends paid by a non-trading parent with trading subsidiaries will not attract the exception because the income in the hands of the parent has the nature of dividends from the subsidiaries rather than trading income and that may well compromise any claim.

In circumstances where a non-trading holding company is involved and is likely to pay dividends while a participator is temporarily non-resident one might consider a corporate reconstruction, probably a corporate demerger involving the split of companies and groups into separate units owned by separate groups of shareholders, where the sums involved are likely to be significant and the participators circumstances warrant it. A reconstruction is complex and requires expert advice to minimise the tax impositions which will arise.

Trusts

The general principle is, of course, that that the recipient should receive the dividend or distribution by virtue of being a participator in the company or an associate of a participator.

So where does that leave trustees who receive dividends from close companies?

Does the anti-avoidance rule apply only where the relevant individual is a participator in the distributing company (which would make sense) or does it also extend to dividends paid to a non-resident trust which then distributes the money as income to the individual which is probably what HM Revenue & Customs will attempt to do in the right circumstances.

If the trust is a fixed interest trust the anti-avoidance rule is likely to apply where the income generated by trust assets accrues directly to the beneficiaries as it arises rather than forming part of the trust fund for later distribution by the trustees. In this event the dividend is likely to be treated as the income of the life tenant, particularly where income is directly mandated to the beneficiaries of such trusts.

With discretionary trusts the position is rather more complex, but since any income distribution is from a source different from the dividend the anti-avoidance rule ought not to apply. A discretionary beneficiary is not a participator and, while the trustees are admittedly often associates of the beneficiary, there is no countervailing provision deeming the beneficiary to be an associate of the trustees.

Trustees of all trusts should keep all existing shareholdings in close companies and new acquisitions of such holdings under review.

Chapter 10 - Writing Off Company Loans

A director may receive a loan advance from his or her personal company provided that it is not in financial difficulty and subject to adherence to the provisions of the company's articles and the 2006 Companies Act.

Shareholder approval, generally by ordinary resolution, is required for loans in excess of £10,000 (the limit is £50,000 if the loan is to meet expenditure on company business, by the way). The board should always agree loan terms and document them accordingly.

An overdrawn director's current account that is not repaid is treated as an outstanding loan and this can create tax complications for both the company and its director.

The company may be subject to a charge, the individual on a taxable benefit on an interest-free loan or a tax a charge write off as well as additional reporting obligations. It should be noted that the March 2016 Budget increased the company tax charge from 25% to 32.5% for loans and benefits conferred after 6th April 2016. This increase mirrors the dividend upper rate to prevent individuals extracting value from their company by means other than remuneration and dividend.

The anti-avoidance provision is specifically concerned with such an outstanding loan being written off by the company. When a close company writes off or releases a loan made to a UK resident director tax charges arise. If the director is a participator the amount released is treated as a distribution. If the director is not a participator the amount is taxable as employment income.

In most small companies the director will be a shareholder and will be entitled to vote at board level and so will be a participator. The distribution treatment will apply to any loans made and written off to the director or his family.

A write off which is treated as a distribution for income tax purposes is treated as earnings for NIC purposes; the write off is not an allowable expense for corporation tax purposes, though the Class 1 NIC paid is tax deductible for the company and any tax is repaid to the company following the release or write off of the loan.

If the company has distributable reserves it may therefore be preferable to declare a dividend and treat the loan as a contra paying the dividend in order to avoid the NIC charge. Conversely, the company can also vote a bonus and treat the write off as earnings. If it does this it will need to ensure that it is mindful of reporting requirements under Real Time Information (commonly known as RTI) reporting for PAYE.

Given these complications, it might be thought that a good wheeze for a participator would be to become non-UK resident for a year or two and then have the company write the loan off. In effect the participator could seek to sidestep the loan write off provisions by being non-UK resident.

This is where the temporary non-residence rule comes in. Should the write off occur during the borrower's period of temporary non-residence, the write off is treated as occurring in the tax year of return.

Chapter 11 – Certain Investments Written as Life Policies

Investment bonds have been available through life companies since the early 1970s if not earlier. An investment bond is basically an investment vehicle offered by life assurance companies, and although really an investment, it does not fall under the capital gains tax regime because technically it is classed as a life policy. Its gains are instead regarded as income and taxable under the chargeable events legislation.

Bond holders are permitted to withdraw 5% of what was invested each year the policy is in force without any immediate liability to tax or having to declare anything on one's tax return, although accurate records of withdrawals are essential. If withdrawals are not taken each year, the allowance is carried forward.

For instance, a non-qualifying policy often takes the form of a single premium investment bond. When the bond is finally cashed in, if it can be arranged to occur in a year when the investors other income plus bond profit does not attract the higher rate of tax, no tax is normally payable. It is therefore generally good practice from a planning perspective to surrender the bond in a year when income is low, say in retirement, or when one is non-UK resident.

Ah ha.

This is clearly income of a type where the investor has control over the date on which the investment can be realised. It is a clear candidate for the anti-avoidance rule.

Before making the surrender, a letter to the life company with which the policy is held is all it takes and they should be able to advise you fairly promptly what the gain will be on making either a full or partial surrender. After all, it is they who will be producing the chargeable event certificate when the disposal actually occurs and it is that figure which will determine the tax payable. In my experience it is wise to obtain confirmation in writing.

For an onshore UK investment bond, if the policyholder is already a higher rate taxpayer in the tax year the gain occurs, he or she pays tax of 20% of the gain with no further liability, the reason being that an investment bond is deemed to have paid basic rate tax at source.

For basic rate and non-taxpayers for whom the 'gain' may push into the higher rates of income tax, they can benefit from top slicing relief. Top slicing relief lessens the impact of the charge at the higher rates and generally the longer the policy is held the smaller the annual equivalent on which the tax charge is based.

The chargeable event gains are assessed against the policyholder's income in the tax year when the gain arises. With some clever planning therefore, one could be a higher rate tax payer throughout one's working life, make 5% withdrawals to raise extra income and then on retirement when income drops into the basic rate band, one could benefit from top slicing relief having had the policy over many years, and withdraw potentially substantial sums without incurring any or very little tax.

Where the policyholder is likely to be a higher rate taxpayer on surrender, he or she can exploit their spouse's basic rate or non-tax status where appropriate by transferring ownership of the bond to the spouse (where they are subject to lower rates of tax) at the time they want to make the surrender. They may then go ahead and make the surrender and the gain is assessed on the income of the spouse. As the transfer of ownership is a deed of assignment by way of gift and not for money or money's worth, it is not a chargeable event.

Similarly, in the case of surrendering a trustee investment one could legitimately sidestep tax by assigning the investment bond to the beneficiaries first, subject to inheritance tax considerations, and then the beneficiaries make the surrender rather than the trustees.

This is all fine and tends to be commonplace planning advice.

Where a gain arises to an individual who is not UK resident, the gain is not chargeable to UK income tax and this, of course, is the point.

Without the temporary non-residence rule it would be relatively easy to arrange to be non-UK resident for a single year, the very year in which a bond matures, and escape UK income tax entirely. If you were to become non-resident indefinitely that is fine but if you are non-resident and also temporarily non-resident, the gain will be chargeable to income tax in the year you resume UK residence. There would be the possibility of an element of non-residence relief depending on how many years you have been abroad.

It has been common practice for certain taxpayers to spend a few years in sunnier climes during which time their life policies are encashed purportedly thereby avoiding UK tax on the chargeable gain. Such a strategy may not be so smart now, if we are talking about less than five years non-residence and particularly where the gain is combined with other income or gains caught by the anti-avoidance provisions in the year of return.

Chapter 12 – Offshore Income Gains (sometimes known as OIGs)

If you own an offshore fund that is not either a reporting fund, or a distributing fund then any capital gain you make on that fund will be taxed as income rather than capital gains, when you come to sell.

That may well mean higher tax than you were anticipating because generally income tax is much higher for most people than capital gains tax, and certainly this is the case following the March 2016 Budget. It is not possible to escape the tax using your tax-free capital gains tax annual allowance and you cannot use capital losses elsewhere to offset the gain because it is not subject to capital gains tax. It is subject to income tax.

Unless the funds are in an ISA or a pension fund, investments affected by this provision will usually be non-reporting or non-distributing funds if they are listed abroad.

But how would you know?

The vital information on a funds status might frankly be buried anywhere, depending on the product provider's whim. The first place to look is on the fund's factsheet or individual web page. The second would be to look for their reporting / distributor status in the prospectus or some other fund supplement. Even then it is not always clear what the status of the fund is as the visible material may merely indicate that forms have been lodged with HM Revenue & Customs. It is therefore always sound practice to check the list of distributor or reporting funds maintained by HM Revenue & Customs to be on the safe side.

The real point is that Regulation 23 of the Offshore Funds Regulations (SI 2009/3001) provides that OIGs realised in the period of non-residence are treated as accruing in the period of return. As simple as that.

As with s 10A, there is an exception for interests in offshore funds both acquired and disposed of in the period of non-residence (Regulation 23A). Regulation 23 in its present form has been in force since 6th April 2013; before then it operated by incorporating the former TCGA 1992, s 10A directly.

Chapter 13 – Certain Pension Receipts

This is another one of those areas where those who have or are retiring to sunnier climes for less than five years might wish to review matters.

A range of pension-related income, lump sums and gains fall within the temporary non-residence rules. Where you receive, or become entitled to, any of these during a period of temporary non-residence you will be taxed as if you received, or became entitled to, them in the period of your return.

These include withdrawals from a flexible drawdown pension fund, certain lump sums paid under an employer financed retirement benefit scheme (or 'EFRB'), certain steps comprising payment of a lump sum relevant benefit (or, for remittance basis users, the remittance of such a lump sum relevant benefit), certain lump sums paid by UK pension schemes in respect of which a charge on receipt is removed by a double taxation agreement and certain taxable property deemed income and gains of a pension scheme charged to tax on a scheme member.

The provisions are quite wide ranging and you should liaise with your pension adviser - probably one with an Advanced Diploma in Financial Planning with AF3 as part of the qualification or the now withdrawn CII (Chartered Insurance Institute) unit G60.

Chapter 14 – Disguised Remuneration

Income taxable under the disguised remuneration rules also falls within the temporary non-residence rules.

The 'Disguised Remuneration' legislation was introduced by the Finance Act 2011. It provides measures to ensure that tax on employment income is not avoided or deferred through the use of trusts or sub-trusts or other intermediaries, for example Employee Benefit Trusts (sometimes known as EBT's) and Employer Financed Retirement Benefit Schemes (sometimes known as EFURBS).

The rules take effect from 6th April 2011 and apply to employment rewards which are earmarked or otherwise made available to an employee on or after that date. This regime was extended in the March 2016 Budget to specifically encompass certain loans.

Example 45 in the RDR3 Guidance is worth reviewing in this context if you may be potentially affected.

It may be anticipated that further sources will be added to this list in the coming years. The full list is found in the RDR3 Guidance at paragraph 6.12.

Chapter 15 – Remittance Basis Users (Non-Domiciliaries)

If you are domiciled in the UK you should skip this chapter.

What is domicile?

Every individual has a domicile. It is not possible to be without one nor is it possible to have more than one domicile at any given time. An individual is often domiciled where they have a permanent home, but not always.

Everyone has a domicile of origin - the domicile with which they are born. Domicile of origin is not necessarily determined by where you are born; instead an individual usually acquires their domicile from that of their father.

Domicile of origin is said to have a strong or tenacious quality and will not change even when an individual leaves the country of domicile of origin to become resident elsewhere. Domicile of origin will remain constant throughout the life of an individual, though it may become dormant by the acquisition of a new domicile of dependency or domicile of choice. The domicile of origin is then in abeyance but it cannot be absolutely extinguished or obliterated. If you doubt the 'stickiness' of your domicile, try convincing HM Revenue & Customs that you are not domiciled in one of the countries making up the UK for inheritance tax purposes!

If you are genuinely not domiciled in the UK but are resident here then it is possible to elect for the remittance basis on your overseas income for UK tax purposes.

Remittances of relevant income and foreign chargeable gains do not in general result in tax unless the remittance basis user is UK resident in the year of remittance. However, ITTOIA 2005, s 832A applies the temporary non-resident rule to remittances of relevant foreign income and requires any such income remitted during the period of absence to be treated as remitted in the year of return.

As with UK domiciliaries this mainly applies to income which has accumulated prior to departure. However, with one exception, it does not apply if what is remitted is income arising during the period of absence.

That exception is concerned with dividends received from non-UK close companies: these are treated as remitted in the year of return if they both arise and are remitted in the period of absence.

The general capital gains tax charging provisions treat foreign chargeable gains as accruing when remitted, with the result that TCGA 1992, s 10A catches remittances of pre-departure gains during the period of absence. Gains both realised and remitted in the period of absence are also treated as remitted in the tax year of return.

Let us run through an annotated example from the RDR3 Guidance to illustrate how this works.

Marie returns to the UK during the tax year 2018/2019 after a period of residence abroad. She originally left the UK to become resident abroad on 2nd September 2013 (end of period A).

She had been resident in the UK for the seven years before her departure and claimed the remittance basis in those years.

While Marie was resident abroad she remitted to the UK the following relevant foreign income:

- £15,000 from 2009/2010 remitted in 2014/2015.

- £18,000 from 2010/2011 remitted in 2014/2015.

- £18,000 from 2011/2012 remitted in 2015 /2016.

- £20,000 from 2012/2013 remitted in 2016/2017.

Total £71,000

Marie therefore remitted £71,000 while she was not resident in the UK but, as she was not resident in the UK, this income was not taxed when it was remitted.

On her return to the UK on 1st June 2018 (the beginning of the UK part of split year 2018/2019), Marie is within the anti-avoidance provisions because her period of temporary non-residence was less than five years.

She will be liable to UK tax on these earlier remittances which took place when she was temporarily non-resident. They will be chargeable to UK tax in 2018/2019, the tax year of her return.

HM Revenue & Customs issued a new version of RDR1 in June 2016 and page 64 draws the attention someone in Marie's position to the above tax implications.

SECTION 3 – THE STATUTORY RESIDENCE TEST REVISITED

Chapter 16 – Passing On

Although not an inviting prospect it is as well to make the briefest of mentions of the position if you were to die while overseas.

You would satisfy the automatic overseas test if:

You died in the tax year having spent fewer than 46 days in the UK and you were not resident in the UK in both of the two previous tax years (or not resident in the previous tax year and the one before that was a split year). This is sometimes known as the Fourth Automatic Overseas Test

or

You died in the tax year and would have been treated as meeting the working abroad test if the conditions were modified to take into account the death (and conditions are met as to residence status in the previous two years). This is sometimes known as the Fifth Automatic Overseas Test.

You would satisfy the automatic residence test if:

You died in the tax year, were resident in the UK for the previous 3 tax years on the grounds of meeting one of the automatic residence tests, the immediately preceding year to that of death was not a split year and when you died you had a home in the UK.

There is no requirement at all that you are actually present in the UK in the year of death.

All this, of course, might only be of interest to your professional advisers and your personal representatives/executors. If you are non-resident the latter should certainly be aware of the implications. It would also affect how your UK tax return was prepared for reporting purposes, of course.

Chapter 17 – Returning to the UK

If your intention is never to return to the UK then this is not an issue …. but many if not most do return even though they may not plan to.

The importance of the returning rules is that which case you fall within will determine the date from which you are regarded as resident in the UK and this will in turn impact on just how long you have been non-UK resident and the precise application of temporary non-residence provisions, where appropriate.

There are five cases to consider and you should be clear as to which one applies to your circumstances.

Case 4 – You were non-resident for the previous tax year and, at the start of the tax year, did not have your only home in the UK, but during the year you did and then continued to have your only home in the UK for the rest of the tax year and, in that tax year prior to that day, you did not have sufficient UK ties to meet the relevant test for that part of the year; for the purpose of this last provision you should substitute the reduced day count limits set out in Table F of the RDR3 Guidance found on page 60. Example 37 of the RDR3 Guidance provides useful clarification.

Case 5 – You were non-resident for the previous tax year and are coming to work in the UK under circumstances where you meet the third automatic UK residence test; for the purpose of this last provision you should substitute the reduced day count limits set out in Table F of the RDR3 Guidance found on page 60. Example 38 of the RDR3 Guidance provides useful clarification.

Case 6 – You were non-resident for the previous tax year because you met the third automatic non-UK residency test, are UK resident for the following tax year (whether or not it is a split year) and satisfy the overseas work criteria for a period from the beginning of the year. The overseas work criteria require the taxpayer to have worked an average of 35 hours a week overseas without a significant break and to have kept days in the UK within permitted limits over a period to the end of the year, but having been UK resident for at least one of the four tax years immediately preceding that year; example 39 should be consulted. In calculating whether you work full-time overseas during the relevant period the 'sufficient hours overseas' calculation is applied to the 'relevant period' but the maximum number of days you can subtract from the reference period for gaps between employments is reduced from 30 days to the permitted limit in Table G which is found on page 65 of the RDR3 Guidance Note.

Case 7 – You were non-UK resident for the previous tax year, are UK resident for the following year (whether or not it is a split year) and have a partner whose circumstances fall within case 6 for the previous or current tax year and the you move to the UK so that you and your partner can continue to live together. For the part of the tax year before the deemed arrival date, you must either have no UK home or, if you have homes both in the UK and overseas, must spend the greater part of the time living in the overseas home; example 40 of the RDR3 Guidance provides a useful clarification.

Case 8 – You were non-resident for the previous tax year, are UK resident for the following tax year (whether it is a split year or not) and from the point from which you start to have a home in the UK, you continue to do so for the rest of the tax year and all of the following tax year.   Example 41 of the RDR3 Guidance provides useful clarification.

So what?

Which case you fall under and your circumstances will affect the date of your return for tax purposes.

All of the situations above are subject to a number of different additional conditions, including rules relating to an individual's residence status in preceding or subsequent tax years.

As you might well expect there is an order of priority to be aware of:

For someone arriving in the UK, if cases 5 and 6 apply and the split year date under case 5 is earlier than the split year date under case 6, case 5 has priority; otherwise case 6 has priority.

If cases 5 and 7 (but not case 6) apply and the split year date under case 5 is earlier than the split year date under case 7, case 5 has priority; otherwise case 7 has priority.

If two or all of cases 4, 5 and 8 apply (but neither case 6 or 7), the case which has priority is the one with the earliest split year date.

You should therefore bear in mind that the date of your return can vary for tax purposes, perhaps significantly depending on which case is relevant and, if more than one, which case has priority.

SECTION 4 – BRINGING IT ALTOGETHER

Chapter 18 – Information, Information, Information

The number one planning point is undoubtedly to maintain excellent and accurate records. My final two tax cases illustrate the point. Although these cases focus on tax years before the new statutory residence test was introduced, they really do demonstrate that the need for detailed records remains paramount.

Many people spend a large portion of the year abroad, but keep ties with their family in the UK. In such cases, it is important that scrupulous records are maintained of not just the date, but the time of their arrival, into and out of the UK. The reason for visits, where they stay and where time is spent outside the UK should also be noted. The extent of record keeping required will depend on individual circumstances, but a full list appears in section 7 of HMRC's Guidance Note RDR3.

If recent moves by HM Revenue & Customs to extend their reach has left the implementation of self-imposed tax exile even harder than understanding the theory, it will undoubtedly be accompanied by ever-increasing numbers for contentious claims of non-residency increasing the pressure on the tribunal and court systems.

Decisions in two such cases – Rumbelow and Glyn, dating from 2001/2002 and 2005/2006 respectively – were recently released by the First-Tier Tribunal: Mr & Mrs Rumbelow lost their case, while Mr Glyn won his. Why were these two results different, and what lessons can we learn from these cases, in a post Gaines-Cooper world and under the new statutory residence rules?

Case 1

James Glyn was in his mid-fifties. He and his wife Sarah lived in north-west London and their two grown-up children had left home. In anticipation of receiving a large dividend from his family property investment company, the effect of which would be to retire from his business, Mr Glyn departed for Monaco with his wife. The income tax at stake was over £5 million. The case concerned only Mr Glyn's residency, though Mrs Glyn's actions and movements would necessarily impact on any decision.

Mr Glyn provided comprehensive evidence with information gleaned from diaries, travel documents and financial records, covering the whole period until his return to the UK in May 2010, shortly after the birth of his first grandchild. He and his wife arrived in Monaco with residency permits, living in an apartment on which they had already obtained a lease, and generally went about enjoying the way of life the Côte d'Azur affords a retired couple with a certain means.

The First-Tier Tribunal found that they had achieved a 'distinct break' in the pattern of their lives, as required by the landmark case of Gaines-Cooper which we have already come across. Mr

Glyn had removed himself from practically all of his UK business ventures, while Mrs Glyn stepped aside from her substantial charity work. They vastly diminished their usual social life in London. They frequently visited the UK (22 short visits, covering 65 days in the year), and on these occasions they stayed at the family home which they had retained – often having dinner with their children. However, the First-Tier Tribunal concluded that the family home was not a 'settled abode' after their departure, and so could not contribute to Mr Glyn being UK resident.

Case 2

Stephen and Pauline Rumbelow were in their mid-forties, and had three daughters – the youngest, aged 15, still lived with them in Cheshire. Intending to make several sizeable property disposals, they decided to leave the UK for Portugal prior to the start of the tax year, leaving their daughter in the care of her eldest sister. The capital gains tax at stake between 2001/2002 and 2004/2005 was approaching £600,000.

In contrast to the evidence provided by Mr Glyn in support of his claim, Mr Rumbelow's approach towards proving his case was summed up by the judge as follows:

"He was not prepared to accept any matter adverse to his case without documentary evidence to establish the matter. By the same token significant aspects of his own evidence were not supported by documentary evidence when we would have expected to see such support."

"Matter[s] adverse to his case" included minutes of meetings with solicitors, and of board meetings of his own company, implying him to be in the UK when he said he was not, and notes of telephone conversations suggesting Mrs Rumbelow was still working in her business in the UK.

When they first 'left' the UK, it was to a hotel in Ypres with a car of belongings, having apparently received last-minute advice that an immediate move to Portugal would have adverse tax consequences. They returned home in May before going on holiday, only securing Belgian residency and a lease on a Belgian property in June – they did not arrive to live in Portugal until the following October.

Unsurprisingly it was held that they had not achieved a 'distinct break' as required. Their house remained a 'settled abode', given their extended 'visits' there – and there was little settled about their residence in Belgium, spending as little time there as possible until they could move to Portugal. Mr Rumbelow kept strong business ties in the UK, continuing to buy plots of land to develop. There was no substantial loosening of family or social ties, in part due to their teenage daughter. In all, it was found there were around a dozen UK 'visits' totaling at least 82 days, including four whole weeks over Christmas, and their absence on a further 62 days in the year could not conclusively be shown: the First-Tier

Tribunal considered that they, "were indifferent...to the nature and extent of their return visits to the UK."

The Lessons

Reading through the judgments, the most striking differences are the approach and mindset of the appellants, the level of detail given in evidence, and the care with which they attempted to divest themselves of their UK residency.

This tax treatment reconciles with a commonsense view of the two situations. In one, a couple have taken early retirement in the comfort of their apartment in the French Riviera, occasionally visiting family and friends back home, until such time as they decided to return to enjoy grandparenthood. In the other, a slightly younger couple have left the country in what appears to have been a hurry with no immediate and fixed plans to settle elsewhere, leaving their teenage daughter behind, and continuing to lead their lives pretty much as before. Add in the differences in quality and quantity of evidence, and it is perhaps unsurprising that the First-Tier Tribunal accepted the former's case and rejected the latter's.

It is also very noticeable that one case undoubtedly involved a medium to longer term mindset; the latter a short term mindset based on personal convenience and personal inclination.

For those who wish to read the case notes you may come to your own conclusions: Rumbelow & Anor v HMRC [2013] UKFTT 637 (TC); Glyn v HMRC [2013] UKFTT 645 (TC).   They are very accessible and make easy reading.

Arguably, we live in more certain times but it should e recognized that the statutory residence test and by implication the temporary non-residence provisions impose substantial burdens in terms of forward-planning and record keeping.

Personal records may need to cover midnights spent in the UK, details of days of presence in the UK, details of days of presence at UK homes, details of days of presence at foreign homes, hours worked in the UK, hours worked outside the UK, etc.

The prudent taxpayer will also retain evidence to back up such records in case of challenge by HM Revenue & Customs.

In my view the clarity provided by the statutory residence test, compared to the old pre-6th April 2013 provisions relating to residence, comes at a huge cost in terms of complexity. It is also my view that the statutory residence test and its anti-avoidance provisions have increased, rather than decreased, the need for those affected to obtain liaise fully and transparently with their professional adviser.

Of course, it may be that the days of becoming non-resident for tax purposes alone are numbered, at least for those seeking to avoid capital gains on property disposals. But what lessons can be learnt by others hoping to prove their case to HM Revenue & Customs and before the courts?

They are simple and straightforward.   Be diligent in following advice, plan and be methodical in your actions, and be meticulous in your record keeping. Or, as Ford Prefect would say: consult the Guide, don't panic, and always know where your towel is.

Chapter 19 – Two Things You Really Should Consider

The Indicator

If you have followed my recommendation and you have excellent records, or will ensure that any omissions or lack of clarity in such records is rectified, then I would then recommend trying out HM Revenue & Customs 'Tax Residence Indicator Tool' as a check to see if you are considered to be resident in the UK from the tax year 2013/2014 onwards for the purposes of income tax and capital gains tax. This may be found at http://goo.gl/yqGOx4

Not unreasonably, the results given rely on you providing accurate information and can only be decided by reference to established facts and circumstances. You have been warned. You may wish to print a copy of the result and keep this for future reference in case of enquiry by HM Revenue & Customs.

It is possible to use this tool retrospectively or to predict what your residence status will be in future years, but what must be understood is that HM Revenue & Customs will certainly not be bound by the results where the information you provide does not accurately reflect your facts and circumstances. The resource is what it says it is, an indicator tool. Do not rely on it but use it wisely.

The Election

The statutory test came into force on 6th April 2013. The anti-avoidance rule does not apply unless the first year of non-residence is 2013/2014 or a later year. The anti-avoidance rule is not given retrospective effect and as a consequence, the residence status of individuals for earlier years remains determined by the old combination of limited statutory rules, HM Revenue & Customs practice and case law. That combination is outlined in skeletal form in the Appendix A.

Since the new rules apply to a person who has been resident in the UK at any time during at least four of the seven tax years prior to departure and who is non-resident in the UK for five years or less, it should be fairly clear that the old rules may indirectly impact on an individual until 2017/2018 i.e. when those who left the UK in 2012/2013, the last tax year under the old rules, have been non-resident for five years.

It is possible to elect out of the old rules in determining residence for any of the five tax years 2013/2014 to 2017/2018. Such an election is on a year by year basis, is irrevocable and must be made in writing. It must be made by the first anniversary of the end of the 'relevant year' in respect of which the election is to apply or, if the year is a split year, the first anniversary of the end of that year. For example, an individual wishing to make an election that their residence status for 2011/2012 should be determined in accordance with the new statutory test for the purposes of determining their residence in 2014/2015 must have made the election before 6th April 2016. For some the possibility of making an election for certain years will have now gone. It is history.

For the avoidance of doubt, the election will not change an individual's actual tax residence status for the pre-commencement year or years nor will it affect their tax liability in that year or those years and knowledge of the old rules remains extremely pertinent in these circumstances.

Chapter 20 – Planning Depends On Circumstances

If you are not caught by the temporary non-residence provisions

If one can stay outside of the anti-avoidance rules then planning is clearly possible, the most obvious example being the ability to delay a disposal which would otherwise be chargeable to capital gains tax by ensuring that the contract for sale occurs or income is received after the date of departure provided you will be staying non-resident for sufficient years. It is well worth bearing in mind that HM Revenue & Customs may be able to successfully challenge the arrangement of transactions if it can be argued that there was, for example, a binding agreement in place before the date of departure. Careful records should be kept if any such planning is undertaken.

Subject to commercial considerations one might also defer certain disposals until you are certain that you could not be inadvertently caught by the temporary non-residence provisions.

Carefully monitor the six year rule to prevent inadvertently being caught by the by the anti-avoidance provisions if you have income or gains which could be subject to UK tax. In other words, ensure that you are genuinely non-UK resident under the statutory residence test and that you do not breach any of the 'day count rules' for UK visits.

Consider selling UK assets owned prior to departure and which are pregnant with significant gains while you are non-resident but not temporarily non-resident. Keep an eagle eye on section 14B of TCGA 1992 if the asset to be sold is residential property and be aware of your reporting and tax obligations to the UK. Carefully monitor your return date if appropriate and indeed the tax regime where you are currently resident.

Watch your return visits to the UK like a hawk. If you become resident for a single tax year this may well have implications for your temporary non-resident status and therefore for your tax and reporting obligations. Simply stating, say, 14 days is not good enough under the statutory residence test if it ever was. You need to know which day you entered the UK and which day you left the UK as a minimum. I would also be clear as to the reasons for each visit and have notes of where you stayed together with appropriate documentation. Remember the two tax cases in chapter 18.

Consider acquiring high growth foreign assets while resident overseas and dispose of them before returning to the UK.

Remember that plans and circumstances can and often do change. You may not have planned to return to the UK but you should factor in the possibility and make contingency plans.

If you are caught by the temporary non-residence provisions

Consider the effect of various sources income and gains all becoming taxable in the year of your return to the UK … a single tax year. The bunching of taxable receipts into one tax year, and possibly a tax year in which you may also have other UK income, could easily lead to a higher liability than would have otherwise been the case. In certain circumstances, being temporarily non-resident could actually lead to paying much more tax than if you had remained in the UK where those income and capital receipts spread evenly over several tax years. It depends on your circumstances.

Subject to the point above even if you are caught by the anti-avoidance legislation it is worth remembering that the period of non-residence still offers the individual a deferral of UK tax until tax year of return. This may be useful if there is only a single event where you are in receipt of relevant income or gains.

While you may not have control over the timing of income receipts, you can nevertheless control when you depart from and return to the UK under certain circumstances for sources on the list in the RDR3 Guidance at paragraph 6.12.

Chapter 21 – The Tax Planners Mindset

At the beginning of this book I mentioned the importance of having a 12 year mindset. Why that should be so should now be a little clearer.

Most people's experience of the UK's tax system tends to be driven by a one year time horizon and that makes a lot of sense. If we submit a self assessment tax return this is invariably on an annual basis. If we run a business or have income from property we similarly account for this on an annual basis. For an accountant with many clients each with their own annual cycles this is equally the case. There is an annual cycle in tax and in accounts, just as there is in agriculture.

When one comes to tax planning the annual cycle and the short term mindset associated with it is rarely relevant, however. For planning purposes it is almost bound to lead to disappointment and frustration. The annual cycle is overwhelmingly a compliance based cycle, nothing more, and adopting it in relation to planning will rarely yield effective results. One needs a longer term perspective to effectively deal with the ramifications of planning and in the case of temporary non-residence that amounts to a 12 year mindset.

Seven of those 12 years are found by looking backwards to the past. If you fall within the anti-avoidance rule then you must be resident for at least four out of the last seven years. You should be able to perform that exercise for every year you are considering.

The five remaining years are found by looking forward from a point where you departed from the UK or intend departing.

You will instinctively know whether you have that all important mindset by considering seven traits. If you have these traits you will have the 12 year mindset necessary to successfully navigate with your adviser across the landscape that is temporary non-residence.

It is that simple, though not necessarily that easy. To that extent the seven traits are also the action points which you should take away from this journey. The answers to that inevitable question, 'So what is the next step?'

Chapter 22 – The Seven Traits

- If you do not already do so, you should maintain accurate records of your time in the UK and overseas. If you do you will not only know where you are with respect to the statutory residence test and the temporary non-residence rules; you will also know how long you should stay in the UK if you wish to remain non-resident for any particular year. If you are already overseas and things are not absolutely clear then this would be a good time to undertake a bit of 'archeology' and piece the picture together. Do your best and share that information with your adviser.

- Be certain whether you are entitled to the split year treatment on your departure from the UK, why and under which case.

- Be certain of the date on which you actually left the UK as well as the date on which you are deemed to have left the UK for tax purposes and why. To do this you will need to know whether you are entitled to the split year treatment or not and, if so, which case governs your date of departure.

- Be certain of your residency status under the statutory residence test for each and every tax year ended 5th April for the seven years prior to departure and, indeed, for any years since you left the UK. If you do not know it is being left to chance and you may have unintended UK tax liabilities and reporting obligations.

- Be certain of whether you are entitled to the split year on treatment on your return and, if you are, which case will take precedence as this will affect the date you are deemed to have returned.

- Be certain of your last year or period of UK sole residence for temporary non-residence purposes.

- Work with your UK adviser on all of these issues. Now you speak the same language and you can appreciate why advisers tend to ask infuriating questions requiring lots of input and, frankly, pain. In short, you can see things from a tax planners perspective ... you have the tax planners mind. Ensuring that your adviser has the numbers to crunch and has awareness of your circumstances is absolutely crucial. Just as the indicator tool of HM Revenue & Customs will struggle to serve you without the fullest information so there is a limit to what your adviser can do without the same resources.

Standing back from everything it is hoped that you now have what amounts to a helicopter view of the rules and practices which govern temporary non-residence. That should enable you to take a realistic view of what you need to do to confirm your status if you are already non-resident and to order your affairs going forward.

Chapter 23 – A Parting Thought

We started out looking at Dave Clark and his landmark tax case.

Things have charged a lot since the 1970's and the biggest change occurred in 2013 - the statutory residence test and the temporary non-residence provisions.

Although many things have changed since the 1970's not everything has changed.

Three things remain the same and, as far as we can tell will never change.

If you do not know the rules and you are leaving the UK for good, never to set foot on UK soil again and you left no UK assets or savings or investments behind, then that lack of knowledge may be irrelevant.

If you do not know the rules and you are doing other than leaving the UK for good, never to set foot on UK soil again, then that lack of knowledge may prove very costly. You cannot plan effectively. The terrain rather than you will determine how your journey ends.

But how will HM Revenue & Customs know about your circumstances?

Simple!

You tell them, and you and your adviser are obliged to do so. It is the law. HM Revenue & Customs are not obliged to guess. Have a look at Appendix C.

If you leave it to HM Revenue & Customs to find out for themselves then you may quickly come to appreciate that transparency is not only the right thing to do, it is also painless compared what your experience of life will become.

However that will not be your fate. The third thing which has not changed is that if you do know the rules and how they impact on your particular circumstances, and that interaction is crucial, then you can be in control of your tax position. You can plan effectively and be 100% compliant. The exact manner in which the rules and your circumstances interact is where the input of your adviser is absolutely essential.   Tell him or her everything.

Spill the beans.

That is what Dave Clark did!

Thank You

Before we part company, I would like to say "thank you" for purchasing my book and reading all the way through it to the end. If you have found this book useful I should be extremely grateful if you would take a minute or two of your time to leave a review on Amazon. It means a lot. Thank you.

No book I have ever read is perfect and this one is no exception. If there are any oversights, omissions or errors or anything you would like to see covered or changed, please email me at stevesbooks@gmail.com.

About the Author

Steve is a writer, blogger and practicing UK tax adviser.

He believes that words can change the way people see the world, their mindset, and that this can have profound consequences.

Mindset may be defined as a particular way of thinking, a person's attitude or inclination about something. Change this, even slightly, and the world becomes a different place.

Appendix A: The Rules Prior To 6th April 2013

The "old" rules will remain relevant for at least a few years, when there is a need to determine whether someone was resident for the purposes of establishing whether they are an arriver or leaver under the new rules (and where no election is made to, in effect, backdate the statutory residence test criteria for this purpose). They will remain relevant indefinitely where those years are, for whatever reason, under enquiry by HM Revenue & Customs, subject to circumstances and statutory time limits.

Example 44 in the RDR3 Guidance may be worth reviewing.

The day count tests are, of course, the basis for the mantra referred to earlier in this book.

Day Count Tests

The 183 Day Test

An individual would always be resident in the UK if present for 183 days or more in a tax year under the old rules.

The only exception to this statutory rule arose where an individual was in transit to another destination via the UK. This meant arriving as a passenger one day and leaving the next, effectively using the UK as a hub to another destination. Where this was the case, the day was ignored for the day counting rules. If, however, the individual attended a business meeting, visited a property owned by them or arranged to meet people socially the day was counted.

Prior to 6th April 2008, it was the stated practice of HM Revenue & Customs in their earlier guidance in IR20 and HMRC6 to ignore days of departure from and arrival in the UK when calculating the number of days an individual spent in the UK. Finance Act 2008 altered this practice to provide that a day was counted if the individual was present in the UK at midnight. Different rules therefore applied prior to the 6th April 2008 counting of days and afterwards.

The 91 Day Test

A further non-statutory test based on HM Revenue & Customs practice took the average of an individual's annual visits to the UK to ascertain whether these came to 91 days or more. The average was taken on a four year rolling basis and if the day count exceeded, on average, 90 days then residence commenced from the start of the fifth tax year.

In calculating the 91 day test HM Revenue & Customs ignored days spent in the UK due to exceptional circumstances beyond the individuals control (for instance, illness preventing travel) providing the 183 day test was satisfied. HM Revenue & Customs used the same statutory definition of a day of presence referred to above when it applied the 91 day test but reserved the right to contest cases where they felt that these were not within the spirit of the legislation.

Special rules applied for employees leaving under a contract of employment that would last at least a full tax year. By concession an individual was held to be not resident if they left the UK indefinitely or permanently or full-time employment abroad which was maintained for at least a year as set out in HMRC6 paragraph 8.5 and ESC A11.

Occasional Residence Abroad

Where an individual left the UK for what was regarded as 'occasional residence abroad' and at the time of leaving the individual was both UK resident and ordinarily resident then they would continue to be UK resident for tax purposes.

Occasional residence was not defined but was generally accepted to catch those who left the UK on an extended holiday or who spent considerable time out of the UK but nevertheless retained a main UK home and UK connections. Accommodation was ignored from 1993/1994 onwards for the purposes of occasional residence.

It was therefore always prudent to consider the quality of time spent in the UK. For instance, although in principle a husband and wife are taxed separately it would be difficult in practical terms for an individual who has lived in the UK with their spouse and children to claim that they had left the UK by virtue of keeping the days spent in the UK within 91 days a year on average.

HM Revenue & Customs practice made it clear that where an individual wished to be regarded as having left the UK, the individual must have permanently left before one could even consider the 91 day test. This is based on much more qualitative and uncertain criteria and tax cases illustrate the subtleties in specific circumstances.

Consequently, where an individual left the UK they would ideally have evidence that they had left for some settled purpose.

If the circumstances of a particular case were outside of statutory rules and HM Revenue & Customs guidance then case law tests existed which could include a range of factors such as the existence of a permanent home (freehold or leasehold), family ties, business ties, frequency and length of visits, nature and purpose of visits and individual circumstances.

Where an individual worked full-time in a foreign employment or a foreign trade non-residence would be more readily accepted.

There was no definition of full-time but it was generally accepted as equating to a typical UK working week. If the individual was away for a full tax year and, during the absence, return visits were less than 183 days in any given tax year as well as being less than 91 days a year on average then non-resident status would usually be accepted.

The concept of occasional residence abroad found in ITA 2008 s 829 did not apply to capital gains tax, since ordinary residence alone rendered a person subject to capital gains tax.

Split Year Concession

Strictly speaking, under the old rules an individual would be resident or non-resident in terms of complete tax years. However, under ESC A11 (superseded by Finance Act 2013, of course) HM Revenue & Customs would operate a split year basis whereby an individual was regarded as resident until the date of departure and non-resident thereafter. The treatment normally applied where the taxpayer:

- had been UK resident but left to live abroad permanently, or for a period of at least three years, such that on departure he or she was regarded as not ordinarily resident in the UK or
- had been UK resident and left to take up full-time employment abroad.

ESC A78 extended the treatment to a non-working spouse.

The Anti-Avoidance Regime Prior to 6th April 2013

Prior to the enactment of the statutory test a similar five year anti-avoidance rule to the current one applied inter alia to capital gains, offshore income gains, and remittances of relevant foreign income (see TCGA 1992, s 10A and ITTOIA 2005, s 832A, both as originally enacted, income withdrawals from foreign pension schemes (ITEPA 2003 s 576A) and UK registered pension schemes (ITEPA 2003 s 579CA). This law continues to apply where the year of departure was 2012/2013 or before.

The RDR3 Guidance Note paragraph 8.11 remains a useful reference where taxpayers are affected by the old rules.

The old law is engaged in any case where the period of absence is fewer than five complete tax years. There was no provision in those rules for calendar years to operate where the former split year concessions applied.

Planning

It is likely that the residence status of any individual for earlier years will already have been determined since the deadline for submitting the 2012/2013 self assessment return was 31st January 2014, the enquiry window for which would have closed on 31st January 2015. This means that there are very limited opportunities for planning for those earlier years.

The well advised may consider making the election protectively wherever the application of the new rules to the prior years will result in them being treated as non-resident for those years for this purpose. It is good practice to ensure individuals meet the statutory non-residency criteria in the earlier years to reduce risk of enquiry by HM Revenue & Customs.

Most elections will therefore no doubt be made where, under the statutory test, the individual would definitely have been non-UK resident in the prior year.

If the making of an election indicates a concern that the individual may have been UK resident in the prior year in question under the old law, albeit that tax returns were not filed on that basis for the year concerned, it would be prudent to check the Form SA109 for each year to ascertain how the individuals status was reported and review the basis for those decisions.

Appendix B: Holdover, Rollover & Deferral Reliefs

The assets affected by these holdover and rollover reliefs are quite wide ranging and the essential circumstances are set out below. It is recommended that you follow the section numbers through a copy of TCGA 1992, as amended:

- assets acquired from another person who acquired them when resident in the UK but did not pay tax on their disposal because of no gain/no loss treatment under the specific rules for husband and wife or civil partner transfers (section 58 TCGA 1992), the death of a life tenant (section 73 TCGA 1992) and works of art (section 258(4) TCGA 1992).

- any interest in a settlement.

- assets which have had their acquisition cost reduced by a capital gains rollover relief being given on the disposal of another asset which had been acquired by the individual while resident or ordinarily resident in the UK.

The rollover reliefs to which this provision refers include:

- compensation and insurance (sections 23(4)(b) or (5)(b) TCGA 1992).
- business assets rollover relief (sections 152(1)(b) or 153(1)(b) (for disposals after 16 March 2005) TCGA 1992).

- transfer of business to a company (section 162(3)(b) TCGA 1992).

- compulsory acquisition of land (sections 247(2)(b) or (3)(b) TCGA 1992).

The capital gains deferral reliefs in question include:

- re-organisations, conversions and reconstructions where the new asset is a qualifying corporate bond (section 116(10) or (11) TCGA 1992).

- compensation stock (section 134 TCGA 1992).

- depreciating assets (section 154(2) or (4) TCGA 1992).

Appendix C: How Does HM Revenue & Customs Know?

HM Revenue & Customs are not obliged to guess your circumstances. Under self assessment taxpayers are obliged to inform HM Revenue & Customs of income and gains whether they are in the habit of preparing self assessment tax returns or not. If HM Revenue & Customs do not know that you have taxable income or gains whether you are resident or not it is because you have not told them. That can carry significant implications unless you take the initiative and report responsibly. If you are approached by HM Revenue & Customs rather than the other way around it is likely that the consequences will eclipse the actual tax due....and I do not merely allude to the financial consequences.

Those who are to become non-resident, whether temporarily non-resident or not, will probably have a final tax return to complete and there will be a return for the year in which they return where appropriate.

Attention was drawn at the outset to the reality that it tends to be those arriving in the country who seek tax advice rather than those who are leaving. However, the well advised may already have appraised HM Revenue & Customs of their plans by one of two routes depending on whether one was within self assessment or whether one's tax liabilities were dealt with under PAYE.

Most, though not all, individuals leaving the UK and who are concerned with temporary non-residence will probably have been registered with HM Revenue & Customs either under self assessment (in other words they submit annual tax returns) or under PAYE. This is because individuals who have the type of assets and income which are likely to be affected by the anti-avoidance legislation will arguably be or have been making submissions to HM Revenue & Customs prior to leaving the UK.

Your Tax Return SA109

If you have been used to completing a self assessment tax return over the years then it is likely that you will have completed SA109 as part of that exercise, particularly if you were assisted by a professional adviser.

The questions relating to your residence status are found on a single page and comprise a mere 14 questions ... but they should not be underestimated. They are extremely well thought through and focused. The answers need to be equally so.

They include questions to establish whether:

- you were resident in UK in the year covered by the return and the previous year.

- you were resident in any of the previous three tax years.

- you have UK ties in the current tax year.

- you meet the third automatic overseas test.

- the split year criteria apply.

- how many days were spent in the UK in the year covered by the return and you have an overseas home.

If you have read the chapters on the statutory residence test you will appreciate that accurate answers to these sorts of questions will give the reader of the form SA109, particularly if the reader is in the employ of HM Revenue & Customs, a very good grasp of your residency status indeed.

If, of course, SA109 was never completed and the view was taken that there was no point submitting a return once you had departed there may be loose ends to tie up and your residency status will be unknown to HM Revenue & Customs.

Form P85

Form P85 is available for those leaving the UK to make a declaration of the relevant facts to HM Revenue & Customs and, although the form is non-statutory, it can be used to reclaim tax mid-year for those not in self assessment.

HM Revenue & Customs manuals suggest that forms P85 submitted for self assessment taxpayers will be rejected. However, many professional advisers will nevertheless submit the forms simply to establish a record of their client's departure with HM Revenue & Customs or they may just complete the form and hold it on file as a contemporaneous record of the facts relating to the departure.

Submission of form P85 should also allow a no tax "NT" PAYE code to be applied to any continuing UK pension income (or employment income where applicable) for departing individuals.

For individuals leaving the UK, where the P85 is relevant, the answers provided to the questions on the form need to be considered carefully and it is suggested that completion by an individual without professional guidance is ill-advised.

Of possible crucial importance may be the requirement that the tax year of departure (or arrivals for new arrivals) qualifies as a split year which, post-statutory residence test, is neither automatic nor straightforward.

An individual may leave the UK part way through a tax year yet easily still fail to qualify for split year treatment for that year as we have seen.

Form P85 is designed to enable HM Revenue & Customs to form a preliminary view as to an individual's residence status and has been redesigned in the light of the statutory residence test.

Some of the questions are, however, somewhat vague and non-technical in form, but they should be considered against the specific provisions of the statutory residence test and not taken at face value.

You may anticipate the following questions:

- How long had you lived in the UK before the date you left (or the date you intend to leave)?

- From the 6th April in the tax year you left the UK up to the date you left were you resident in the UK?

- How many days do you expect to spend in the UK between your date of leaving the UK and the following 5th April?

- How many days do you expect to spend in the UK in each of the next 3 tax years?

- Which country are you going to?

- Will you (or your spouse, civil partner or someone you are living with as a spouse or civil partner) have a home in the UK while you are abroad?

It is not uncommon to find that SA109 or P85 has not been completed.

This is partly because either form requires considerable precision in the answers and a certain understanding of the residence rules. Not completing these forms is not necessarily a problem depending on the circumstances but it does also mean that there may be a lack of definition in determining precisely when a person has left the UK, whether they qualify as non-resident and what they should be doing or not doing to maintain and preserve their status. The issue has only been deferred.

These forms set out your stall to Revenue & Customs and there is a clear need to monitor your days in the UK, their quality and the number of ties you have. There are others. Even if the forms are not submitted there is no better way to address the issues and focus the mind than by drafting your answers to the questions these two forms pose.

Printed in Great Britain
by Amazon

86373378R00088